Stella's Sisters

Voices from Moldova

Philip Cameron

As Told to Nancy Silvers
and Brian Paterson

Dedication

To all the other Stellas trapped in the hell that Moldova reserves for its orphans, cast out onto the streets with no help, no hope, and no future... This book is written for you, that you would no longer be forgotten. To you we pledge our determined efforts and fervent prayer that you will never again be without a home to call your own.

**"I assure you!
Whatever you did
for one of the least of these...
you did for me!"**

Matthew 25:40

Moldova

International boundary
County (județul) boundary
★ National capital
⊛ County (județul) capital
Railroad
Road

Chisinau is both a county and a municipality
Gagauzia is an autonomous territorial unit
that is not coterminous.

0   20   40 Kilometers

0   20   40 Miles

Lambert Conformal Conic Projection, SP 48N/45° 40'N

FOREWORD BY NANCY SILVERS

It seemed a typical Sunday morning as I entered the expansive sanctuary of New Life Christian Fellowship in Jacksonville, Florida, in August 2009; but my world was about to be radically changed! As I took my usual seat, the worship team was already beginning to sing. I perused the church bulletin. Philip Cameron was to be the guest speaker that day along with his girls from Moldova.

Moldova? I pondered. Where is that? Philip Cameron? Of the famous Scottish Cameron family who brought the first praise and worship songs to America back at the beginning of the charismatic movement? My brother and I had worn out their records playing songs like "All Over the World" and "The Dancing Heart."

What is a man from Scotland doing with girls from Moldova? I wondered.

Then, when Philip took the microphone, he explained about the little country Moldova that very few people notice in the world except for one group — slave traffickers! And then he told us he was turning over the platform to the girls.

I shifted indifferently in my seat as the teen girls, dressed in black t-shirts and pants, gathered on the platform. I was simply not prepared for what followed as girl after girl stepped forward to give her testimony, telling about horrors and a struggle to survive that I could not have imagined if I tried! With each progressive story, my heart felt gripped until finally tears spilled out, accompanied by sobs and crying from parishioners seated around me.

Quite simply, I have never in my life been so captivated or moved as when these young girls shared their life stories. And I knew when they were finished, that I had to do something, anything, to help Philip Cameron save these girls and girls like them from slave trafficking. Philip had reluctantly gone to Romania at first, simply because God told him to go. Once there, however, his heart had become captured by the deplorable conditions of the orphanages and the forgotten children. A part of him wanted to walk away, but he could not do it. Instead, he stayed and what followed were miracles, miracles in Romania and then in Moldova.

God took one man, Philip Cameron, and turned the darkness of destitute orphanages into light. Holes in the ground became real bathrooms; dilapidated windows which literally froze the children in winter became modern sealed glass of protection; moldy walls became clean and fresh; group showers became modern individual shower stalls; totally cold orphanages became warm for the first time with modern heating units; moldy wet beds became lovely modern ones with clean mattresses. As Philip shared with the Body of Christ what he was seeing, the Hands of Christ brought what was needed.

And then Philip took on the slave traffickers. Since the girls are turned out of the orphanages with nowhere to go, the orphanage directors and slave traffickers, in league with each other, then sentence the girls to more horrors than even the orphanages had given them. But Philip intervened by building a place called Stella's House, named after a young girl who was turned out of a Moldovan orphanage and then abused by men until she died of AIDS. "Never again!" seems Philip's motto as he takes on this battle to save the girls from the streets and the traffickers!

Hearing the girls' stories of the horrors they endured until Philip Cameron's saving hand pulled them up out of the darkness shook me so hard that Sunday morning that I knew I would never be the same. I knew I had to do something to help, and, partnering with Philip Cameron, this book has become my contribution.

For three absorbing days, I interviewed Natalie, Galina, Constantia, Irina and Dasa, listening to and recording their compelling stories. And now I offer them to you. I have tried, as much as possible, to render the stories to you in the girls' own words. But be prepared! Once you read them you cannot stay the same!

At the end of the summer, Philip and the girls had an opportunity to meet Jim Caviezel, the actor who played Jesus in Mel Gibson's *The Passion of the Christ*. The girls had seen the movie, so they felt overwhelmed to have their picture taken with "Jesus."

"Jesus called me a saint," Philip jokingly told me, explaining Jim Caviezel's words to him after the picture. The pastor at Frazer UMC in Montgomery, Alabama, had just told Mr. Caviezel about Philip and his work at Stella's House.

Yes, I thought to myself. Philip, you truly

are. For Stella's Sisters is actually two stories: the girl's story, of course, but also the equally riveting story of how God took one willing man and brought innumerable children out of darkness into His marvelous light.

Nancy Silvers
Script A Life Author

TABLE OF CONTENTS

**Philip, Chrissie Cameron
Stella's Sisters from Moldova**

"We met the children and knew God had sent us into their tragic world..."

Philip Cameron

INTRODUCTION

For eleven years, I diligently told everyone I knew that two children were plenty in this day and age. My wife Chrissie and I watched Philip and Melody Joy grow up together, and our little family was truly complete, or so we thought. Then came a trip to an orphanage in Romania, and we adopted our precious Andrew. A little over a year later, we experienced the most wonderful surprise of our lives when beautiful Lauren Anne was born.

I'm thrilled to tell you, though, that our little family just seems to keep on growing. The kids you'll read about in this book, and many others with them, have been inextricably knit to our hearts in ways I still don't understand. I know God loves them and never stopped caring for them, and somehow He put them in our hearts so that we would feel just a little of what He feels for them. When we met them, they were lost little souls, with not a single flicker of real hope within them. But that was not the end of the story, and the hope that flows today in a place called Stella's House is as astonishing as it is palpable.

Touched by the lives of five of these extraordinary girls, Nancy Silvers helped me tell their stories with incredible skill and sensitivity. My friend and colleague of thirty-five years, Brian Paterson, also helped me put on paper a little of the amazing journey that took us to the orphanages of Romania and Moldova and to the miracle of Stella's House. I'd like to offer them both my sincere gratitude.

I mentioned the word "miracle," and I know it's a word that gets overused, but as you read on, I trust you'll agree its usage is entirely appropriate here. And so I'd like to thank the God of miracles for all the wondrous ones He has given us on our way.

Philip Cameron

NATALIE

Lovely Natalie Gutium was born into this world on June 20, 1991, in the town of Calarasi, Moldova. Sent to an orphanage of seven hundred children, Natalie, being only seven years old, felt overwhelmed and lost. Would she never again be loved by anyone? Here is the moving account of her story.

In my life before the orphanage, when I was four years old, my mother became blind. My mother, at 24, suddenly could not see at all, and I remember wondering if she would ever be able to see again and worried she might die. She was sick and could not take care of me, so she gave me to my grandma. But it was very hard even then because there was no food or bread. We had to go into the woods to find mushrooms to eat. My grandma decided then it would be better for me in the orphanage because I would have a bed and food to eat. Even though the orphanage did not have great conditions, Grandma thought it was a place where I could be safe.

So Grandma gave me to the director of the orphanage, a place where my uncle, Nicolae, my mother's brother, already lived. And I remember thinking, What's with all these kids? It seemed like a village of kids, and I couldn't understand what was going on.

I was seven years old, and I knew that at seven years old, I would have to start going to school, so I asked my grandma if this was the school where I would be going.

"Yes," she said. But I couldn't understand because this place was an hour away from my grandma's home.

"How am I going to be able to come home every day," I asked her, "when it's so far away and we don't have money for a bus?"

"You're not going to come home," she answered simply. "You're going to stay here, and I'll come visit you and so will your mother."

My biggest fear had been about my mother. I was only four years old when she had given me to my grandma. Now, three years later, it was hard to even remember my mother's face. And I wondered, How can my mom visit me here, an hour away from Grandma's when she never visited me at Grandma's, a place where Mom could have walked to?

Fortunately, my Uncle Nicolae was at the orphanage with me. He was five years older, and he took good care of me. He used to wash my clothes, and if someone tried to hurt me, he would step in and protect me. My uncle always told me, "You know how our house here is like an animal's house. Do you want to live like that?"

"No," I replied. It wasn't just about the things we didn't have. It was about not having a family that forced me to listen to his advice.

"Well, if you want to get out, you have to learn and be good in school. Because if you learn and be good at school, you can get a job."

After he said that, I tried very hard in school to get good marks. I did it for him. I didn't really understand at the time everything he was talking about. And really I didn't feel any hope of being anything in life, but my uncle pointed out how the government was paying to support us.

"You can't live like that!" he told me. "We have to step up and give ourselves a chance to live."

I lived in the orphanage for nine years after Grandma left me there. And I would go with my best friend Dasa to the orphanage gate. When Dasa first came to the orphanage, I told her how I always walked to the gate to look for my family to come for me.

"Well, I can come with you," she said. So that's what we did.

We would stand at the gate and just look up and down again and again, all day long, the day ending with me crying, trying to find an excuse why no one came.

Probably the bus isn't working. Maybe they don't have any money. I tried to make up excuses all the time. I didn't want to consider that they just didn't want to come, that they didn't care.

Life at the orphanage was pretty bad. With seven hundred kids, no outside organization would help us because there were too many orphans! When they came, they would ask, "What do you need?"

Our director would reply, "Well, anything you can help us with!"

Then the organization would reply, "We can help with shoes. How many pairs do you need?"

"Seven hundred," came the answer.

"Seven hundred? Sorry. We can't help you then." And they would leave.

During the night we would sleep three or

four girls together, especially in winter time because it would get so cold, and we were afraid we would freeze! And we didn't have any warm water, so we had to take showers in cold water! Looking back now, I wonder how we kids could have ever lived like that! At night I used to lie in bed and cry, because my future looked so hopeless.

After I had to leave the orphanage, I moved into a room with my friend and her mother, but the place was infested with bugs!

I couldn't get into college, so I went to a Sports School; and I still remember when I went to get my documents, there was this woman who asked me, "What do you want to be?"

"I don't know what I want to be," I answered, "But I want to get into college."

"What are your marks?" she asked, and I gave her my average.

"Well, I don't think you can get in," she said.

"We don't have better opportunities to get in because I'm an orphan?" I asked plaintively.

"Well, what do you expect?" she answered harshly. "Do you think I should pay for your school?"

"No, Ma'am" I said politely, although very hurt. "That's not what I ask."

That was my first experience in the real world, and I had been rejected. I tried to stay tough, but it hurt me deeply. So I took my exam and entered the Sports School since it was the only school open to me. And I stayed with my friend in her bug infested room battling the bugs that were everywhere, even in our food. Then the director from the orphanage called me.

"Remember those people who put new windows in our orphanage? The people who came and talked to you?"

"Yes," I said. "I remember them." When I first left the orphanage, they told me they wanted me to come and live in a place called

Stella's House, but they did not have enough beds for me to go there right away.

"Well, they have made more room at Stella's House," the director said, "and now they have a bed for you. You and your friend Dasa can go there if you like."

Dasa and I were so excited! When we went to Stella's House, the people there had food for us, beds, even pajamas, jeans, and clothes! They also gave us school supplies because up to that point, we hadn't been able to afford basic school supplies.

I remember when I first opened the door, Stella's House was so beautiful that I hesitated even going in, stopping to take my shoes off.

"Don't take your shoes off!" the friendly people told me from inside the house. "Come in as you are! Leave your shoes on!"

But it looked so clean! "No," I insisted, "I have to take my shoes off." I cried so hard as they showed me my room and my bed. It was a miracle! As an orphan, when I had been asked about what my dreams were, I had none because I knew I was just an orphan. Orphans can't even dream. And now here I was in this wonderful place!

I stayed in Stella's House for a year, and it was more than a house, food, and a bed to me because there I also received love. And there I received my first Christmas gift. Mom and Dad (Chrissie and Philip Cameron) had brought us so many presents!

I said, "You've gotten me so much stuff. I don't know where it will all fit!"

Dad responded, "Well, I talked to some people in America about you, and they wanted you to have these presents."

The American church people had sent us coats, shoes, jackets, and jeans. At the orphanage I had had one pair of jeans, and that was it. Now I had several pairs to choose from! Oh, we felt so spoiled!

And when we first took showers at Stella's House, we would take forty minute showers! Then Dad said, "Girls, if twenty girls each take forty minute showers, how much water will you spend?"

But we would laugh and say, "But, Dad, it's been sixteen years. We haven't had showers like this. We're making up for all that lost time!"

Stella's House completely changed my life. I never knew God, and I never dreamed He was using everything to help my life. My biggest fear as an orphan was that I would grow up, have children myself, and they too would end up in the orphanage because that is what we were told would happen to us. They repeated that message to us at the orphanage over and over again. And it was so hard being a little girl and then a teen, a time when I needed a mom, and yet had none. How I needed someone to tell me what girls needed to know. I needed someone to tell that I was special and not a mistake. My mom was living her terrible life, I told myself, because of me!

Last summer (2008) when I came to America, I could not believe what I saw! The roads were so smooth, and the large trucks seemed so cool. I had never seen something like that before! During my first experience in an American restaurant, a buffet, Dad told us we could go back and get more food.

Then I asked, "If I have salad, can I even get some fruit?"

"Yes." He said. "Of course, you can go get fruit!"

Unbelievable! I thought.

In America, as I shared my story, I was deeply moved as people accepted me. I was so afraid at first that I would be rejected, but Dad said, "I promise you they'll never reject you. They'll accept you as you are. They'll be more than happy to hear your story."

It was the first time I felt unashamed, the

greatest feeling in my life!

Another thing I noticed right away in America is that people smiled at me. When we went to Wal-Mart, the people seemed so friendly and always smiled.

"Why are the people smiling?" I asked Dad.

"Because that's the way people are here," he explained.

In Moldova, no one ever smiled at me. They despised us, hating all orphans!

When I went back to Moldova, I went to see my mother, and when I saw her living conditions, I cried and prayed to God, feeling how unfair it was that now I was living such a good life while she didn't even know what bread was. I know she put me away, but after what God has put in my heart, I didn't want to hate her. During the summer in America, some people had given me money, and I had saved it so I could buy my mother something. And that's what I did. I bought her food and just tried to give her a little bit of the good things I had.

She started to cry and said, "I'm sorry. I'm sorry for the life I gave you. I know you didn't deserve it. I know you deserved a better life. I've gone through hard times as well."

My biggest goal now is to help orphans like me. I can stand up and tell them, being an orphan myself, that they are special and can do better in life. I can tell them that I came from the same orphanage they came from, and I know exactly how they feel and what they're going through. I want everything I do in life to glorify God. I want to choose life, not death; and God is life.

My message to you, the reader, is never to give up in life, and it's never too late. I had thought my own life was too late to change anything, But I was wrong. Jesus died for me and you.

I am a giver, and I like giving to help

others. Dad helped me take my mother to the doctor last spring, but the doctor said he could not help because the blindness is from something inside her brain. During the visits, she stayed with me in Stella's House; and she slept with me two nights and then started to cry.

"Whatever you do in life, do everything you want to but don't do something that will waste your life because I did mistakes and how I've wasted my life," she told me.

I believe, however, that it is not too late for her. I want her to believe in Jesus. I want her to change her life. She was depressed after the doctor's report, but I love her and want her to know she is not alone.

My Uncle Nicolae became a Christian while attending a Christian camp in Moldova. I was a teenager, sixteen, when I first noticed it. It was meal time, and I noticed his head down; so I asked him, "What's wrong?" Then I saw he was praying. He told me then that he had accepted

Christ at a camp. This brought a big change in him because before that Nicolae had been so hungry for things in the world just like me as a teenager. But now he was definitely different. I did not understand it at the time though because I had not yet come to Stella's House. But he gave me a Bible for kids, and I did read it.

As an orphan I believed there was a God, but I did not put my trust in Him because I did not know what trust was and did not trust anyone. But when the Camerons came to the orphanage, they were so different from anyone I had ever known! Then during my first week at Stella's House, Dad was trying to explain to us in our own language what the love of God really means. A woman stood next to him, translating for us.

"Here's you," he said holding out his right hand, "and here's Jesus," holding out his left hand. "And I'm God, and I look at you and at Jesus and decide to give Jesus for you."

But I'm nothing! I thought to myself. Why would He do it? I'm just a sinner. Why would God do this?

"Because He loves you," Dad explained to me.

And then I got it. I felt His Presence throughout that service and received His love. Dad and Mom's loving example also helped me understand God's love for me. And the many people who give to Stella's House to help girls like me, even though they cannot visit to see for themselves, show me His love as well. I can see now that God has always loved me and used even the orphanage to bring me to Mom and Dad Cameron and the new life I am living today.

GALINA

Beautiful Galina Telescu was born in the northern part of Moldova, in Basarabeasca, a part of Moldova with a large Russian population. Coming into this world on July 19, 1988, little did Galina expect the cruelty that awaited her. Here is her moving story.

My parents divorced when I was four, and they took me then to my grandparents and left me there. But my grandparents could not take care of me because my grandmother was sick, so my grandparents put me in an orphanage, and I stayed in that same orphanage for eleven years because the director of the orphanage did not know if someone was going to pick me up some day. That also meant I could not be adopted, because no one from my family had signed permission papers so that I could be adopted. I never saw any of my family again. They never came to visit, and they did not even call. I quickly lost all contact with them, and after a while I could not even picture them. After eleven years, the orphanage director finally moved me to another orphanage, Cupcui, located outside the Moldovan city of Leova.

At the first orphanage, all the children spoke Romanian, a language I had never heard before! I was told I had one summer to learn the language before school started in the fall! The director of the orphanage was teaching me, but it was a lot of work for a little four-year-old girl like me; and she would beat me if I did not learn quickly enough, shouting at me for being too slow. This did not seem normal to me because I was just a little girl, and she seemed so mean, not nice at all. Somehow I did learn to read and write Romanian but still had trouble speaking it.

When school started on September 1, students from the orphanage went to public school with the other students in town, but once there, it was a horrible experience because the village students made fun of us orphans. No one seemed to care that this happened, not the orphanage director or the adults over us. It seemed we were just a job assignment to them. They did not truly care about any of us.

After school we came back to the orphanage and had lunch, but if an orphan came too late to lunch, no food would be there at all. They would take my food and put it into a bucket to take home at the end of the workday to their cows and pigs. I would have to wait until dinner for food because orphans had no snacks.

And the conditions at our orphanage were really bad. We had a leaking roof and no bathroom or showers inside. After lunch we would go upstairs to our beds and find them wet from the rain leaking onto them. Often, even at night, we would try and move our beds to avoid the leaking water, but usually our beds and thin mattresses were still wet.

Then we did hours of homework, and next

came our chores. Sometimes we were assigned to clean the kitchen while other times we cleaned other rooms. The orphans cleaned everything in the orphanage.

Often we had no light, so during those dark times they could not make us dinner, so we would get only a slice of bread and some juice. And it was very cold, too, because there was no heating system. Every bed had only a small blanket and pillow and one thin mattress, so we would put beds together and huddle ten girls at a time to try and stay warm.

Finally, the director was removed from her position. They discovered that she was stealing clothes and other items that were supposed to be given to us orphans; so they got rid of her. The new director, Gheorghe Antoniu, was a kind man who tried so hard to help us, but his job was overwhelming! The conditions were so bad that not even animals could have survived since it seemed colder inside the orphanage than it was outside!

As an orphan I had one pair of shoes, one pair of jeans, and a couple t-shirts. I never owned my own clothes. We did not even have a warm coat. And when we washed our clothes each week, we would have to wash them and then choose something out of the pile to wear for the week.

We never celebrated birthdays and never had a toy or a game. We had television in our classrooms but really never got to watch anything for very long. We never saw cartoons or even the news to know what was going on in the world. We had textbooks and could read storybooks in the library, but usually we would take a book and go together to a room where one of the girls who could read would read aloud a story to us. If we had any free time, the orphanage teachers would take us to their homes to work in their fields so that they did not have to work. At Christmas we would celebrate with a concert but never were there any gifts. We would be divided into two groups and sing to each other in this room as our performance, but the only people there to hear us sing were the teachers and the director, never any parents or family who cared about us. Only the teachers, who did not want to be there, attended, always staring at us with their evil eyes. I can still picture them, their hard eyes watching us!

Afterwards, we went back to our cold rooms. We had to have a shower once a week. The showers were always cold water, and we had to walk to another building outside to take them. We often got sick because it was so cold. But there was nothing we could do about it because there was no health care, and we could not afford a hospital because the director had no money.

The toilets were outside, too, and if I woke up in the night, I'd have to ask someone to go with me because there were no lights. The toilet was fifty feet outside the orphanage building, and never was there even any toilet paper! Every day seemed like a fight to survive in the orphanage.

At fourteen, my eyesight got bad, but no one would take me to see an eye doctor. My eyes got worse and worse, but no one cared. I became very scared, afraid I would never see again! It got so bad that finally I could not even see. I certainly could not see the board at school, and then teachers started calling me "stupid," telling me I would never be anything significant; and I started to believe them since that is all I heard every day.

Back at the orphanage I would help other girls with their homework, and they then would get good grades; so I wondered why people thought I was stupid! I yearned for someone to take me to the eye doctor! At night I always needed help to get to the bathroom because of my eyes, and, thankfully, one friend, Constantia, helped me out.

One Christmas concert, however, some

strangers came in just as we finished and asked us to sing again. Normally we just sang to each other. I had never seen such happy people! We were surprised but thrilled that they wanted us to keep singing for them. The happy people were Philip Cameron, his son Andrew, his daughter Melody, and some other church people. They could not speak our language, but we understood their smiles and hugs; and they gave us stickers, our first presents ever! We could tell they actually cared. From that night my life totally changed.

Philip Cameron put windows, heating, and showers in our orphanage; and when we came back after the summer (because all orphans leave the orphanage in the summer to work in the fields for villagers), we were thrilled to see a real indoor bathroom, showers, and windows.

I actually thought I was dreaming! We walked into our bedrooms and saw new beds with thick mattresses, new sheets, new pillows, and new warm blankets. It was gorgeous! We were not going to starve or freeze anymore!

A lot of times I had cried, thinking my terrible life was normal; but now I knew it was not. I felt I hated my mom, my parents, especially when I found out from the director that my mom and dad lived nearby with my three brothers and two sisters. I had been the only child my family gave away! And now I could not even remember what they looked like. It hurt me so bad! I just could not believe that they did that to me! I had a picture of myself when I was little, and I looked cute, not ugly. So why did they abandon me? It would make sense if I had been ugly or something deformed. But I was a cute child. Why then? And I used to ask God why I had to go through all this and live in such a terrible place. If God loved me, why did I have to suffer all this?

When Dad (Philip Cameron) came to the

orphanage, he asked what was wrong with me; and the people at the orphanage told him, "She's stupid!"

"No," Dad challenged. "Something is wrong with her!"

I finally was taken to a doctor, who did a brain scan and found a tumor, explaining the problem with my eyes; but Dad did not tell me what the doctor found. Instead, the Camerons tried to take me to America for surgery; but it is difficult for an orphan to get a visa until eighteen, and even then it is not easy. I had to wait three more years, often feeling dizzy and not well. I did not know the problem, of course, and when nothing happened after visiting the doctor, not even glasses, I felt that no one cared.

When I turned nineteen, I had not finished high school. I had only completed sixth grade because of my eyes. I got my visa though and went to America for my surgery. Still, I felt terrified.

I had known Philip for five years at this time, before he built Stella's House. We orphans were so grateful for what he had done for our orphanage, and we asked him if we could call him "Dad," and Chrissie "Mom." I had been an orphan for fifteen years and thought I would never have parents again. I always thought I would end up on the streets and be homeless because that is what we had been taught by the orphanage. But here was this loving couple who said, "Sure. You can call us Dad and Mom!"

When Dad would ask us orphans what we would like to be, we would always say, "We want to work in the kitchen!"

"In the kitchen?" Dad would say. "But you could be anything you want. Why the kitchen?"

And we then explained to him how if we worked in a kitchen, there would always be food, so we would not starve!

In America, however, a lot of people were praying for me as Dad traveled to churches and told my story; and when I came to America for surgery, the doctor there did another scan and found a miracle! The tumor was gone! So instead of surgery, I was given glasses. It was like discovering another world! I could see what was riding down the street! I used to have headaches and dizziness. I had just needed glasses!

I asked Dad why he did not tell me in Moldova that I had a tumor, and he told me he did not want me to worry. He said that he and Mom had already decided that they would take care of me for the rest of my life, if needed. I could not imagine people loving me so much! They had been complete strangers, but they loved me!

I had a Bible written in Romanian but always felt confused about God. But God transplanted my heart once I came to know Him. I knew God had healed me in America. I learned English there and listened as Dad preached to me a lot, going through the Bible; and every word he said touched me. I felt like God was there too each time Dad told me about Jesus, and I just cried and cried. And then Dad would pray for me every night and tell me how much God loved me. I was full of hate before, but knowing Jesus has changed me completely. I found the most amazing love in Him. I realize now that I'm special. I feel that God had me go through the horrors I did so that I can now help other orphans like me.

Today Constantia and I go back to the orphanage and do puppets, manicures, and other fun things for the orphans like Dad did for us. To go there, though, brings back a lot of bad memories because the same teachers and workers are there, so something inside of me yearns for them to see me as special. Look how far I've come, I feel like telling them! I hated that place so much; I only go back there for the girls and boys to tell them there is hope for them and to give them encouragement. When we share the Gospel, while Constantia talks, I look out for the teachers because they will not allow us to share Christ.

One time I was in the same room I was in as a kid, remembering the freezing cold nights, the black mold covering the wallpaper, the leaky roof; and it was so hard to be there with those memories, but now the Camerons and Christ have changed all that for me.

Stella's House is a great opportunity for us girls. We can go to school and have Bible studies. I'm very thankful every morning I wake up because I am so blessed. And I tell Jesus, "Here's my life." I know I have to move forward. For everything He's done in my life, I have to give back. I do not want to live my life without blessing others.

To you, reading my story, everything I have shared is from my heart. If you feel God talking to you, pay attention and do not ignore it. If you want, God can change your life. He changed mine. And if He leads you to do something for Him, do not wait until tomorrow. Do it right away. Even though I did not finish high school, I think I can do anything through Christ. With God all things are possible. I am planning to get my visa for America next year to go to Master's Commission. After that I will do whatever He wants me to do.

Looking back, I feel glad my parents abandoned me. I pray for them and would like to meet them one day. I would like to hear my mom's story about why she abandoned me. To get my passport, I needed a new birth certificate so I went to my hometown, and the government official there told me that my family still lived in that village. Dad (Philip) then said, "Let's go see them."

But I said, "Not now." I do not know what I was thinking. I guess it was all hitting me. My heart had just melted with the news that they still lived nearby, and I was not ready to see them that day; so we returned instead to Moldova's capital city, Chisinau, and Stella's House. Some day I do want to see my mom, however, and tell her about Jesus. I know she is very religious, Russian Orthodox, but she does not know Jesus.

I realize though how very fortunate I am because I met the Camerons and became part of Stella's House. Many orphan girls in Moldova feel lost and aimless when they are kicked out of the orphanage at sixteen. This is when the slave traffickers offer them jobs. In the orphanage we were never taught about the dangers outside in the world, so young girls are easy prey for the slave traffickers. The girls only know they need a job and will go wherever needed in order to survive. Two girls who went to the same church as I were offered jobs when released from the orphanage and traveled to Atlanta, Georgia, thinking they were going to get jobs in America. Once in Georgia, however, they realized the jobs were not real and fortunately managed to run away to a house on the street whose residents took them in. I actually met these girls when I myself came to America, and they asked me why I was not afraid of Philip. Then I told them my story, and they envied me, wishing they had known him too.

Thank you for reading my story. I hope it will bless you. Thank you so very much.

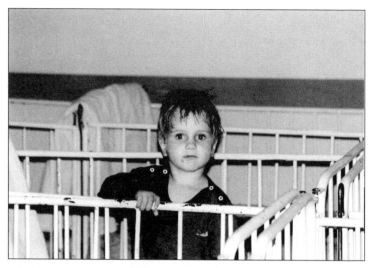

Timisoara, Romania. 1990. In the first orphanage Philip visited, he found this little boy, then four years old. Within a short time and after an amazing series of events that can only be called miraculous, Philip and Chrissie adopted him, and Andrew William Cameron became a much-loved member of the family.

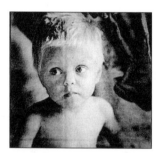

This picture of a little girl called Marina appeared in a British newspaper under the headline, "The Dying Rooms of Moldova." Shortly after, Philip made his first visit to Marina's home, the orphanage in Hincesti. The horrific conditions there sparked a mission of mercy that continues to this day.

This is Constantia as she was when Philip found her. Here she is seen sitting on her filthy bed in the orphanage at Cupcui. Constantia was there when Philip Cameron Ministries rebuilt the orphanage, and continued to live there until she moved to Stella's House.

Left: Philip stands in the one shower stall that existed in the Cupcui orphanage. It was located outside, far from the main building where the children slept. The children were given one five-minute shower per week in freezing cold water.

Below: Ancient, poorly functioning boilers that dismally failed to properly heat the children's rooms in Cupcui.

Above: Clean, modern, well-heated restrooms with plenty of hot water for daily showers were installed on each floor of the building when the Cupcui orphanage was rebuilt.

Below: A brand new heating system was installed to stave off the brutally cold temperatures of the Moldovan winter.

Above: Exterior of the Cupcui orphanage after rebuilding, complete with new roof. The old roof leaked so badly, they said, "When it rains outside for a day, it rains inside for a week!" The interior rooms were so cold and damp that dangerous black mold grew on the walls, inches from the faces of sleeping children. No more!

Below: Philip with some of the kids from Cupcui.

CONSTANTIA

On July 19, 1990, stunning Constantia Sacalova was born in a village in Moldova called Frumusica, near the city of Leova. Left at an orphanage when she was only four years old, Constantia struggled to survive until one day her mother appeared at the orphanage to get her. Here is Constantia's story of struggle and survival.

When I was four years old, my father was murdered by some older orphan boys as my father came home with his sheep that day. The boys robbed my father of the 150 rubles he had with him and beat him. My father was beaten so badly that he lay where the boys had beaten him for three days in the rain before finally managing to get home. My mother knew something was wrong when the sheep came drifting home without him. When my father finally arrived home, my mother took him to the hospital, but it was too late by then, and he died in the hospital.

After that my mother simply left me at my grandmother's house, so my grandmother, being too poor to support me, eventually put me in an orphanage. It happened right after my father's funeral when my mother just walked away. After two years without any word from her, my grandmother told me my mother was dead and took both me and my sister Cristina, who was six and half years old when our mother left us, and placed us in the orphanage. I had one other sister, Carolina, but she was older and lived in the Ukraine.

Grandma had been nice to Cristina and me, but there was never enough food. Often we ate the chicken's food, taking the corn and boiling it, so we could survive. On rare occasions we would actually eat a chicken. So at six years old, I, along with my sister, was put on the bus that took us to the orphanage to live. I was too young to understand what was happening to us, so I chattered to another young girl my age on the bus; but Cristina understood and cried. The girl I chatted to was called Irina Lazar, someone who would become my dear friend one day, but I knew nothing about that then.

And then there we were, in an orphanage that held so many kids!

At first, seeing so many kids, it looked like maybe this place could be fun, with so many children to play with. Within three months, however, I soon realized that the place was not fun. My sister and I were separated because of our age difference, sleeping in separate places. This bothered me because I was put in a room with kids I did not know. It was a cold, miserable place where water poured on my face as I lay in bed, the leaking roof dripping down on me when it rained.

Then one day, when I was seven years old, my mother showed up at the orphanage and called me to come to her. My sister Cristina had already spotted her and had run to her room to escape my mother, but I was totally caught off guard as she called to me where I stood outside.

She looked horrible, her face swollen and bruised, and I felt terrified! My grandmother had told us our mother was dead, and here now was this scary woman calling to me, saying she was my mother. I did not want to go to her and tried to run, but she paid some of the older orphan boys to get me; so off we went with her to the Ukraine, to a convent in a town where my oldest sister Carolina lived.

My mother had gotten a job at the convent, and we lived there for four years; but I never went to school. Instead, I worked with my mother, usually looking after the sheep and cows, a job I learned to do after watching other girls tending the animals. We had a room and food, but unfortunately, my mother was an alcoholic; and when the people at the convent found out, they kicked my mother and us out.

Back in Moldova, my mother found a man to live with, but he did not like kids, and when my mother drank, he did not like that either; and so often he would kick me and my mother out in the middle of the night into the street. I was eleven years old then and should have been in the sixth grade. My mother had many different boyfriends, and they all beat her; and sometimes we would have to go outside and hide in the corn because she was beaten so badly. We were often very hungry. I remember how I had just one pair of boots to wear that were too small for my feet, so I had to walk in them with my toes scrunched up inside.

My mother continued to drink and get in trouble with different men, and I remember running at night into a field and lying down in the grass with my mother to escape these different men who were coming after her. Once a knife landed by us. These men never beat me, but it was a terrifying existence.

Once we worked for a lady, both my mother and me; and we each earned 60 lei (about $5). And my mother asked for the money I made working since she had already used up her money. I had given my money to my cousin, however, with the hope of getting to my sister in the Ukraine; so my mother kicked me out on my own because I would not give the money to her. I then went to my cousin's and lived the summer with her.

My aunt was a government official, like a mayor, and she obtained documents for me to go back to the orphanage. By this time I had lice, so no one at the orphanage wanted anything to do with me. I remember crying, embarrassed, in the middle of the dormitory room because no one wanted me. That is when a girl, Galina, offered to let me sleep with her, lice or not. The supervisor, when she heard this, said to Galina, "Why would you do such a thing?"

Galina, knowing Russian, helped me with

Romanian while I helped her with her blindness, helping her get to the bathroom in the night.

As mentioned before, I should have been in sixth grade but was so far behind in school by this time that they put me in the beginning grades so I could catch up. The little kids made fun of me, however, because I was so big, so I hated both the orphanage and school. Finally, they put me in sixth grade. I would memorize a poem to learn, or copy homework, trying to keep up. I kept wondering why my family put me in such a place. I concluded that it was because I was ugly and stupid.

The building was freezing cold, and for showers five of us girls had to shower at once in cold water with no hair dryer and no nice warm clothes to put on when we were done. We had very little clothes, and we had to look after them because that little is all we had.

The orphanage roof leaked every time it rained, making our beds and mattresses wet.

And the walls were covered in black mold. No one came to visit or help us because there were too many kids, and there are so many orphanages in Moldova; so it is just too much for anyone to help us.

At our Christmas program, I would try to imagine my mother being there, watching me, being proud of me; but no one but the teachers ever came, and I could tell from the teachers' faces that they really just wanted to go home and be with their families for the holiday. And so when the singing program was over, attended by our mean teachers, I would go back to my room and cry. My heart felt a dark black. I felt hopeless. I did not know about God. I did not know He cared for me and was watching over me. I felt alone, in despair.

One Christmas was different, however. I was twelve at the time, and we were singing as usual to each other the songs we had learned, accompanied by our music teacher who played an accordion. Then in walked Philip Cameron, his daughter Melody, his son Andrew, a doctor, a pastor, a Scottish man, and a woman we came to know as Auntie Mary. Surprisingly, they asked us to sing again, and they all seemed so happy.

Why do they care? I wondered, mystified by these joyful people. We are just orphans, and no one cares for us. We had been taught that no one would ever care for us, and we would never be anybody. Little did we know that on that very day, Dad Cameron was preparing a contract with the orphanage director, Mr. Gheorghe, to repair our orphanage.

And then they gave us Christmas gifts: stickers that they placed on our faces! But it was more than stickers they gave us. They gave us love and hugs!

The following summer Galina and I were hired out to work for villagers just as all orphans were, since the government did not want to pay for us in the summer. And when we came back to the orphanage in the fall, it was like we were dreaming! The Camerons had fixed our orphanage! We had warm water, new beds, and heat! We even had a bathroom and individual showers! Nice new thick mattresses were on our beds and fresh pillows, sheets, and blankets! It was a miracle!

And Philip himself came to play games with us! And he brought us clothes and more hugs. He told us about the love of God. That is when we asked him if we could call him "Dad." We were thrilled when he replied, "Yes!"

Will he come back though? I wondered. After being treated so cruelly, it was so hard to believe this man really cared. And then it was time for me to leave the orphanage. I had nowhere to go. I took my exam but did not know where I would be going. My only dream was to work in a kitchen, so I would not starve!

With nowhere to go, I felt scared. But Dad wanted to build a house for us since something bad had happened to another girl when she left the orphanage. Going to Stella's House, I never had to worry after school about what I would eat or where I would go.

Dad then told us, "I love you this much," showing us with his hands, "but Jesus loves you this much!" And he spread his arms wide. And he showed us a movie about Jesus. None of us said a word as we watched, enthralled by how much God loves us. And I decided to give God my life since He had brought me to this wonderful house and provided me with a loving mom and dad (Chrissie and Philip Cameron).

If I had not come to Stella's House, I would either be married to a man who mistreated me, raising children who would end up in the same orphanage I had been in, or become part of the slave trafficking. I hate the devil for doing that to young orphan girls because we never were treated right and never knew that worse evils awaited us once we left the orphanage. It is not right that young girls have to go through that!

Now I love to go back to the orphanage, the same one I came from, to the same bed, and tell the girls what God has done for me, to give them hope. I, like them, had thought everyone hated me; and so I hated everyone else in return. But Mom and Dad Cameron really changed my heart. And while I was learning English, I wanted to tell the Camerons so badly how much they had helped me, but I had trouble finding the words. I finally managed to tell them, "My heart was dark. It was black. But now because of you and the grace of God, I am new."

Today I tell orphans that they are special. I especially love sharing with the handicapped girl orphans. One girl, Vera, really touched me when she asked me if God would accept her because of her deformed body. And when I explained to her how much God loved her, she then asked me that if I should die first, would I please ask Jesus to come get her because she does not want to live in the handicapped orphanage any more. The handicapped never get to leave the orphanages in Moldova. This brought tears to my eyes. Vera loves Jesus very much and enjoys singing praise songs to Him! She even got baptized. I love telling the orphans stories, giving them hope.

If you, the reader, do not know Christ, He wants you to know Him. And if you happen to go through something terrible like I did in life, I hope you realize that you're not a mistake, and God has a plan for your life. And if you hate someone, it is time to forgive and see God's plan and His love. I thank all the people who are part of Stella's House, who sacrificially have given their money to change an orphan's life. I pray that God will bless them back even more than what they have given!

DASA

Darling Feodocia Rosca, known as Dasa, came into the world on April 7, 1991, born to a family in a village called Sireti in Moldova. Abandoned first by her mother and then her uncles, Dasa was left to survive in an orphanage in Moldova, wondering if she would live or die. Here is Dasa's story.

My dad left my mom when I was born, just because I was not a boy. After that, my mom took care of me for two more years, but then she left me with my uncles and went to Russia to work. After a few years, my uncles put me in an orphanage, Straseni, where I spent seven years. My heart and my world soon became empty. I was so sad, wondering all the time just one thing, Why can't I just die? I did not know Jesus, and so I did not know anyone cared for me. I never even knew my dad.

Every night lying in my bed, I thought of

my parents, crying till my pillow got wet. So many times I tried to imagine my dad coming to visit me. I wanted so much for him to come and take me home. I dreamed of him spending time with me, loving me. But it was nothing more than dreams.

My birthday still seemed special to me, and I yearned for family to be beside me, to feel that kind of love which only a dad or mom could give me. All my life I wanted just three things: to have a dad, a dog, and a bicycle.

All the time, especially when feeling sad and forgotten, I would put my head down and try to dream again. This time my dad was really coming to take me home, and for my birthday he was giving me a dog and a bicycle! I pictured him spending time with me, playing with my dog. There I was inside this beautiful house, hugging my parents.

I wanted so much to hear them saying "Happy Birthday." I lived with beautiful dreams but nothing more. I asked God so many times "Why did you make me? Why me? Why isn't my dad coming to kiss me before I go to bed? Why is he not here to spend time with me? What did I do wrong?"

Sometimes I was so worried about my life, and I started to think how to change my life. But because I was an orphan, most of the time it was easier for me to choose to be a bad orphan rather that a good one, since no one ever said anything positive to me. I used to think, I have to hate all the people around me just how they all hate me!

Most of the time a voice inside me stopped me, saying, "Your life is in your hands." And again then I started to dream of my future. But then, looking in the mirror, speaking to myself, I would say to my reflection, "You are so ugly! You are stupid to dream. You are only one more orphan in this world. Nobody needs, cares, or loves you. You can't have a normal future like kids with parents do! You have to die. This world was not made for you, and you don't have a space here!"

Then I would cry, asking God to take me from this world. "I am nothing, God. I will never be good enough to do something with my life!"

When I wanted to forget all the pain, I would read. I lost myself in books, forgetting all about my world as I entered a fantasy world. When I was reading, I forgot all the things that made me feel like nothing, alone, and forgotten.

Every Sunday I continued to wait for my mom to come and visit me, standing at the brown orphanage gate with my friend Natalie, the scene still vividly etched in my mind. She did not come, of course, and so I would run back to my room, crying in my bed till the morning came and a new day started.

Everything seemed the same every day. Sometimes I wanted just to sit down and never get up again. I was so tired of my life, being left with only my beautiful dreams.

I never trusted anyone. I had a motto "No one can love you because you are an orphan," and all the time I followed this motto. I seemed broken, so I never could belong to somebody. But in just one day Jesus changed the rest of my life.

One week before I was to leave the orphanage, I met the Camerons. Being sixteen, I was about to be turned out of the orphanage with nowhere to go. Philip and Chrissie Cameron had put new windows in the orphanage for us, a real blessing, and were visiting the orphanage that day to see the finished work.

I was busy cleaning my room since I was going to leave, but then the director called some of us older girls down to the office. Seated on a bench with the girls, I met the Camerons who said they were building a house for us.

It was not ready at the time, so I lived three weeks with my mom and her husband in the city, but it was a hard life because her husband was always beating me. But then the director from the orphanage called and said there was a place for me and Natalie at Stella's House.

That is how God made my dreams become a reality in just one day. He miraculously sent me a mom and dad. He even gave me a house, better than I ever dreamed! But the bad voice inside me did not want to leave me so easily, so I started again to feel like an orphan, thinking that I did not deserve to be a part of a family. I cried most of the time.

When Daddy (Philip Cameron) spoke to me, he always said, "You are special! You are beautiful! You are important, and I love you."

Looking at him, I would cry, thinking in my mind, What do you see in me to love? I am nothing. What did I do to deserve your love? I cannot believe or trust you. My mom told me the same, and where is she now? One day you will disappear just like her!

But Daddy spoke to me every day. He told

me about Jesus, and how much He loves me, how important I am in His eyes. I started to think about this, asking myself, How can somebody love me? How can somebody think I am special when I am not? No, this is not real. I will never be loved.

I was trying every day not to think of this, and all the time I was trying to push these thoughts out of my mind. But all the time when Daddy spoke to me, he spoke directly to my heart, and I could feel my heart softening, responding every day. Daddy brought light in my life.

Inside me was a fight, but I am happy today that the good part of me won. I started to trust Dad and Mom (Philip and Chrissie Cameron), and soon I realized how it feels when people around me actually love and care for me. Jesus made my heart new; He changed my way of thinking; He changed me. He opened my eyes and my heart. Every day I have a new love for Him.

Daddy and Mom are my angels because they made me believe in myself, in my future; and they made me understand that I am not a mistake but created to fulfill a great plan. I know Jesus loves me just as I am, and I am happy He brought me into His world. I see now that it was His Voice encouraging me in that dark orphanage to hold on. He helped my friend Natalie and my cousin Nadea as well.

To you, the reader, I say, this is not about a story but about a life that has been changed because of His grace. Listen to His Voice because He wants to speak to you all the time. Believe that He has His Hand on your life and do not keep Him only for yourself. Tell everyone around the world about Him. What I have been through makes me realize how many more are like me. It goes deeper into my heart every second that there are no orphans in God, but we must tell them this!

I am not an orphan any more! Oh, I

mentioned I always wanted a dad, a dog and a bicycle – and that's exactly what I got! I have a family here and a Heavenly Father Who loves me!

IRINA

Precious Irina Lazar entered this world on March 23, 1992, in the town of Leova in Moldova. With her mother's death and her father's alcoholism, Irina, a kindergarten student, just six years old, had nowhere to turn. Here is the stirring account of her life.

My mother died when I was just a little girl in kindergarten. They told me my mother had water on her lungs, and three months after she went to the hospital, she died there. That left me and my three brothers and sisters to be raised by our father, but he had an alcohol problem, and we were very poor. It seemed like the worst time of my life.

My mother was a wonderful woman. Everyone in the village thought highly of her. Even when she was sick, she had worked hard to buy food and clothes for us. Then, when she was sick in the hospital, she still thought of us, delighting us with toys and clothes when she could. But my father said terrible things to us when my mother was in the hospital, how he hoped she would die soon because he was sick of us and wanted to get rid of us! This kind of talk terrified us.

At school my elder sisters always wore beautiful clothes, and village children there played with us all because we wore nice things and had nice school supplies. Teachers too were pleased with us because Mother never was late paying our school tuition.

But when Mother became ill and her brother took her to a hospital in Chisinau where she died, our lives took a terrible turn.

I remember at the funeral how we all cried, but my father laughed, being drunk as usual, acting like the happiest man in the world! It felt like the most painful day of my life, especially because after the funeral my older brothers and sisters left me and my two sisters with my dad while they went to live somewhere else. That meant my father could beat me and my sisters, and no one would help us! I was just six years old when my world came crashing down on me!

There had been some pictures of my mother on the walls of our home, but my father burned all but one of them. Fortunately, he didn't burn the last one, and actually after a while, still drunk, seemed to miss my mother and would cry when he looked at her picture. But he often beat me and my sisters.

He would leave the house early every morning, telling us the jobs we were supposed to do while he was working in the fields, warning us to stay inside while he was gone. After he left, however, we often went outside anyway to play; but, sadly, no children now wanted to play with us because we were so poor, and our clothes were no longer nice.

When we saw him from a distance, coming

home over the hills, we would run inside and hide under the bed to escape the beatings that were sure to come.

The children at school now called me names because we were so poor, singing an insulting song about us. It hurt me so bad since I was just a little girl and could not understand the drastic change in my circumstances. I hated going to school then and one day stayed home, hiding under the bed until my sisters came home from school. It was a terrible way to live, not even being able to ask my father for food! He always seemed drunk, and while occasionally he actually treated us decently, most of the time we cowered in fear under the bed, sometimes for days at a time, when he was in his drunken rages!

The mayor in our village saw our condition and decided to put us in an orphanage in Cupcui. I, being in kindergarten and just six years old, felt more than happy to leave my father, but my sisters did not want to go to the orphanage because, being older, they knew it was an end to any hopes to be respected by people. Once an orphan in Moldova, you become like trash to people.

I liked the orphanage at first, even though the conditions were terrible, because there were a lot of children to play with. Our food was particularly terrible, often containing worms, and our dormitory had mold-covered walls and wet beds from leaking roofs; but I seemed to adjust to these horrors. But I felt lonely in my heart, without love or care from anyone around me.

After just three months in the orphanage, however, my uncle came and adopted me to work for him since he had no one to help him. But he wasn't respectful to me, and it was very difficult keeping up with my schoolwork because I had to work so many hours for my uncle. So my schoolwork was suffering, and even though I was living with family, my aunt and uncle did not love me or even seem to care about me.

I would come home from school with a lot of homework and try to work on it, but then I also had to take care of the animals, the cows and horses, and also do chores like shelling corn. I managed to adjust for the first year, but then, for some reason, my aunt and uncle began suspecting that I was a thief!

I remember one time in particular when my aunt was missing twenty lei (about $2), and she thought I took it. She later found it but never apologized. Then she said she heard something in the night, a noise coming from the kitchen. I was in my room praying, but she came in and claimed I had been in the kitchen stealing.

I was just a little girl, but they beat me, causing me to feel terrified around them. My uncle would smack me really hard, and then I would retreat to the kitchen to my aunt, but her response was always to hit me as well. And because I fell behind in my schoolwork because of the work I had to do each day for them, my aunt then called me "ugly" and "stupid," making me feel even more isolated and alone.

I wanted so badly to prove to them that I could work hard, to have them love me, but it never seemed like I could do enough. My aunt used to threaten me that if I did not please her, I would be taken back to the orphanage where I would have no family. So I tried working harder to please her, afraid any minute they would both turn on me and take me back to the orphanage.

But it was so hard each day getting up, going to school, and then coming home to eat and work. I tried to fit time in for school, but I could tell I was falling behind.

My teacher at school could tell something was wrong, but I could not tell her what my life was like. I believe she cared and wanted to help me, but I was too afraid of losing my family and home, no matter how terrible the conditions.

Then everything changed one day. My uncle worked as a security guard, and I went to where he worked to give him bread and soup that day. I was only seven years old at the time. Suddenly, he grabbed me, tickling me at first, and then sexually attacking me. Fortunately, my aunt walked in on him, causing him to stop. She then threatened him that she would go to the police if he tried that again. Looking back, I would think she would have been concerned for me, but she was not. Never did she act like she cared about me.

I remember once when my cousin came to visit that my aunt hugged her and showed her a lot of love. How I watched in anguish, wondering why my aunt could not show me the same affection. She then suddenly turned to me and said, "If you do what you're told and do good in school, maybe you will deserve some day to be loved!"

After my uncle's attacking me, however, I was soon taken back to the orphanage. So, at age nine, I was brought back to the orphanage, forced to leave behind any semblance of family I had known, feeling all hope inside me leaving as I entered the dreadful orphanage. And I felt then rejected and unloved, without hope of any real family.

Some girls at the orphanage treated me kindly, but the conditions were very bad inside the orphanage. We always seemed to have water on our beds and tried moving our beds around to keep them dry, using wash basins to catch the dripping water; but we also had no heat or warm blankets. Sometimes we stood against the wall, the only warm place in the room, trying to get warm.

They put me in fourth grade, but I was so far behind that it was very frustrating. My teachers called me "stupid" because I did so poorly. I kept praying just as I did at my uncle's, but I had no idea who I was really praying to. God seemed far away from me in that place.

One Christmas, however, Philip Cameron, whom we called "Dad," came and showed us love for the first time. But I did not understand why he acted so kind and felt sure he would never come back. But he did not visit only once but many times, each visit drawing me closer and closer to this man who seemed to really love us! And then he told us how he was building a house for us, so that we would not be out on the streets ever again.

When I first entered Stella's House, it was such a beautiful place. It seemed like I was dreaming! Stella's House seemed like a castle to me! And they gave us clothes, new jeans, and coats. I could not remember having such nice things! I still could not understand though why these people were being so nice.

Constantia tried to get me to go to her Bible study held there in the house, but for a while I managed to make up excuses not to attend. But finally I found time to attend and ended up praying with her after she shared how much Jesus loves me. Then when I visited America in the summer of 2008, I got baptized at Rock Church in Huntsville, Alabama.

Stella's House totally changed my life! I no longer had to worry about what I would eat or where I would stay! Today I hope to study and become an English teacher to help the girls and workers at Stella's House with their English.

To you, the reader, I would like to tell you to never give up and always trust God because there is always hope!

THE STORY OF STELLA'S HOUSE

The Dying Rooms

There it was again. The icy wind bit at my cheeks, just as it did every time I went outside. It was almost mocking me, daring me to escape from its merciless blast. Another freezing gust hit my face, forcing me to turn my head away and hurry as best I could to the shelter of the doorway.

I don't know if I've ever felt so cold, yet I stood there, knowing that once I turned the door handle, I could never go back. I would be involved, I would lose my claim to innocence; I would have no choice but to act.

It wasn't as if this was the first time. Seven years before, as I sat in the comfort of my den watching the evening news, the phone had rung. I knew who it was. He called every night at the same time.

"Hi, Dad," I said cheerily. Dad loved good news, and I always tried to have some ready for him.

It was about 5:35 pm in my home in Alabama. In Scotland, it was six hours later, and Dad was getting ready to go to bed. My dad was Simon Cameron, a spectacular preacher whose eloquence in the pulpit and mastery of the language were extraordinary, but in these nightly chats, he was content to use the soft dialect of his upbringing in Northeast Scotland.

"And fit then? (And what then?)" he asked.

In other words, he wanted to know what was going on in my world that day. More precisely, he wanted to know what was going on in our ministry, what were we doing for the Lord. It was a question he asked me every day of my life.

At the time, I was thirty-five years old. I'd left Scotland and established my own ministry. I was a successful evangelist, preaching all over the world; and I'd had the privilege of ministering alongside some of the most famous names in the Church. But at these moments, Dad wasn't impressed by any of that. With those three little words, he was holding my feet to the fire, making sure I wasn't getting off track, making sure I still knew what I was supposed to be about. And he wasn't about to be fobbed off with generalities. He wanted details, numbers, results. He wanted to get inside my head and weigh what he felt from my spirit. It was an implacable level of accountability that I needed and cherished, and, wise man that he was, he knew that.

Our nightly ritual had become even more precious to me lately. Dad had been diagnosed with a large melanoma on his back; and he was having trouble healing after the surgery to remove it. The wound had burst, and in order to try to get it to heal, he had been trussed up and ordered not to move. Basically, he was propped up in his chair with a pile of pillows, with not much he could do except read and watch the 24-hour news channel on satellite. I was just glad that they'd caught the thing, and that they thought they had managed to remove all the cancerous cells. Dad listened to me talk for a while, and then he asked me a question that, to me, seemed way out of left field.

"What do you know about Romania?"

I didn't know much. "That's where that gymnast comes from, isn't it? You know, Nadia Comenici."

The silent pause told me Dad was unimpressed.

"Haven't you been watching the news? It's terrible there right now."

With his satellite, Dad could watch the same news broadcast from ABC News that I watched in Alabama. Sure enough, there was an item that night about unrest in Romania. It was

December 1989, and the world had just watched in amazement as seventy years of communist rule came to an abrupt end in country after country in Eastern Europe. The Berlin Wall crashed down under the weight of the hopes and dreams of millions, people who would no longer live without freedom. The Iron Curtain all but evaporated. Almost overnight, the world had changed.

But Romania was different. This was no bloodless transition. Nicolae Ceausescu, the dictator who had ruled Romania since the end of the Second World War, was determined not to give up power. His secret police, the Securitate, were shooting at people in the streets. They knew that if Ceausescu fell, they would be next. They hoped their terror tactics would cow the people into compliance, but it was too late for that.

For the next few nights, Dad and I watched that ABC broadcast together, and began to sense that this was more than some passing interest in a news story for Dad. On Christmas day, the news came that Ceausescu had been executed for his crimes. It was a grisly end, but it was hard to feel much sympathy for a man who had inflicted decades of cruelty and hardship on his people.

With that, the news stories largely went away from American screens, but in Britain, the BBC and others began to uncover the extent of Romania's suffering. Dad continued to sit in his chair taking it all in. He would call me, sometimes raging that these things could happen, sometimes weeping over the sheer scope of the tragedy that so many Romanians had endured.

Then came the final straw. "Philip!" He was weeping profusely. "Have you seen what they've done to the children?"

The news coverage in America hadn't yet gone into this much, but on the British news they were watching horrific pictures of kids being discovered in Romania's orphanages. The conditions these children were living in defied belief. Little emaciated kids were shown lying in their own waste, covered in sores, rocking themselves constantly, utterly bereft of care or comfort.

"We've got to do something about this, Philip."

I almost fell over. "We! What do you mean, we?" I gasped. "You're sick and I'm busy. Exactly what do you think we can do."

I tried to evade the subject with some humor. "Anyway, when you say 'we,' you really mean 'me!' "

This was a running joke with us. Dad used to say, "Why have a dog and bark yourself?"

There was only one thing I could say to that: "Woof!"

Dad played along with the banter for a second, but then he got deadly serious again. "I mean it, Philip. I can't sit here and know those children are suffering like that. I have to do something."

In all honesty, I just wasn't interested. I was truly sorry for these kids, but the most I wanted to do about that was to send a check to World Vision or one of the other "big" organizations who do this sort of thing all the time.

"Dad, there's nothing we can do. My calendar really is full for months, and there's no way you can travel with your back the way it is."

I should have known better. The one way to get my Dad's motor running was to tell him there was no way to do something.

Then the shameless manipulation began. I say that with tongue-in-cheek, but Dad knew exactly what he was doing. "Well, I'll go myself then. I already told the church that we were going to start gathering food to take to the orphanages."

Only then did Dad tell me that on the

previous Sunday, he had taken a small plastic bag of canned goods to church with him. He put the cans on the pulpit and told everyone that these were just the first, that he wanted everyone in the congregation to start bringing their own cans and other food items to church, and that that they were going to collect as much food as possible for the children in Romania.

I knew I'd already lost the argument. I moved my speaking dates around and found two weeks to go back to Scotland and drive the 2,800 miles from there to Romania with my dad. As far as I was concerned, we'd drop the food off and turn right back round again. I'd make Dad happy, drive those 2,800 miles back as fast as I possibly could, fly home to America, and then I'd be done with Romania.

What I didn't know was that Dad had gotten a whole publicity machine going in Northeast Scotland, both in our hometown of Peterhead and in the region's biggest city,

Aberdeen. A local reporter got a hold of the story and led with headlines like, "Cancer-Stricken Pastor Plans Mercy Mission to Romania."

A local food manufacturer donated tons of cans of food. The area's main hospital donated huge quantities of baby bottles and formula. When I arrived in Peterhead, Dad took me over to see the supplies coming in. One of the biggest buildings on our ministry campus is called the Relfe Center. Usually, it served as a canteen and recreation area and an activities hall for church functions.

I couldn't believe my eyes. Mounds of supplies were being sorted by hordes of scurrying volunteers. There wasn't a square inch of available floor space.

"Dad, this is amazing. I can't believe you've collected all this stuff."

Dad looked at me strangely for a second, then he smiled. "No, Son, you don't understand. This is only what has come in today. The rest is already in the trucks."

"Trucks—what trucks?" I gasped. I knew we didn't have any trucks. I thought we'd be pulling a little trailer full of stuff behind Dad's vehicle.

"Oh, we've got the use of a big rig with a double trailer, another big furniture truck, and a few smaller vehicles as well." He was grinning by now. He was enjoying putting one over on his skeptical son.

Dad had put together a bona fide aid convoy and had set the entire area buzzing with his plan to help the children of Romania. It was an amazing sight to see. All day long, people drove up with their bags and their boxes, just as thrilled as they could be to be doing just a little bit to help these kids.

I've never been so proud of my dad as I was right then. He's always been my hero, but here he was, still sick, still hurting just to walk around, but full of purpose and determination and, in stark contrast to my own approach, already making a huge difference in a tragic situation.

Dad went easy on me though. He was glad I was there, and I was at last getting into the spirit of things with him. A couple of days later we set off down through Scotland into England. We took the ferry across the English Channel, and then on to the long haul across the roads of Europe. First Belgium, then Germany, then Austria, then out of the European Union countries (at that time) into Hungary. At the Hungarian border, customs procedures really kicked into gear and we waited in line for hours on end. Finally, we made it into Hungary, only to go through the whole dreary process again a few hours later at the Romanian border.

Once we made it inside Romania, it was like stepping back in time. It was already dark, but we drove through towns and villages with not a single light on. The roads were unlit, too, the surfaces potholed and scarred. Someone had the idea of painting white lines on the trees by the side of the road, so that at least there would be some approximate clue as to where not to drive.

We finally made it to the city of Timisoara, the largest city in the country other than the capital of Bucharest. We found a hotel. This was no cheap place—it cost us foreigners about $70 per room, a pretty good sum at the time. But expensive or not, it was a complete shambles. There was one single working light bulb—not that it mattered since the power was out most of the time. There was some running water—but only from the cold tap. And the cold was starting to get to me. No matter what I did, I just couldn't get warm.

We had been given the name of a church in the city, and that became our distribution point. For the next few days, we gave out tons of the food and other supplies we had brought, and I was starting to feel like things weren't going to be too bad. Sure, the people didn't have much, but help was flowing in now and slowly, things would start to get better. Dad would be satisfied, and soon we would all be heading home.

Dad was having none of that. He asked every person he met about the children he'd seen in the pictures on the news. It dawned on us later that most people in Romania had no idea this was going on. It certainly didn't fit in with the image of the ideal communist paradise represented in Ceausescu's state-run media. And up to a few weeks before, no one in the outside world had any idea what was going on either. Finally, someone said that they'd found an orphanage. It was literally just a few hundred yards down the street from the church, but they had simply never noticed it was there.

Something gripped the pit of my stomach. I didn't know how, but I just knew that everything was about to change.

We pulled up in the courtyard of

Orphanage No. 2. That's all they called it. Orphanage No. 1, we later discovered, was in the center of town, but this was a smaller facility, home to about two hundred kids.

From the moment I stepped out of the vehicle, I knew I hated the place. "This is your idea," I told Dad. "You go and look around, and I'll wait here."

Dad just looked for a second. Nobody orders me around, not even Dad, but sometimes he just knew he was speaking for a higher authority and he did so without hesitation. "You're coming in."

Oh, how I wanted to argue, but deep down I guess I knew who was really issuing the instructions, so in I went.

I felt absolute, tangible dread as we walked into the orphanage foyer. I was getting in way too deep, way too far out of my comfort zone, and I knew — don't ask me how but I knew — that I'd just crossed a threshold from which there would be no turning back.

I wasn't two feet into the room when I started to gag. The stench was overwhelming. Human waste, years of filth upon indescribable filth, bleeding and sickness, hunger, horrific poverty, desperation, deprivation and death — it was all communicated in that vile, unbearable smell. After some introductions, the staff began to show us around. I could tell you that the sight of those sad, suffering children melted my heart and that was all it took, but that wouldn't be true. I was desperately sorry for them, and I wept my way from room to room, but in my heart of hearts, I just wanted to get out of there. We gave the orphanage director all the food and supplies we had left, and Dad was busy promising that we'd send more help soon; but I wanted nothing to do with it.

It was too hard to watch, too hard to see this much suffering concentrated in these few little rooms. The children were crammed in like animals in cages. There was barely enough room to walk between the rows of rusty metal cribs. We later discovered that their cribs were covered in dangerous lead paint that that many of the children gnawed on continuously. They rocked themselves constantly, the only comfort available. Human contact was almost absent from their lives. If I put my hand near them, they'd hold it hungrily to their cheek, completely desperate just to be touched.

I got out of there as quickly as I politely could. Dad got in the vehicle and I said, "That's it. I did what you wanted, and now we're leaving... And I'm never coming back!"

I couldn't sleep all night long. Every time I closed my eyes I saw them... rocking. Very early the next morning I woke everyone. "I'm leaving in thirty minutes. If you are coming, be in the van."

I was determined to put as much distance as possible between me and what I'd just seen. I drove across Europe like I was a hunted fugitive, stopping only where I had to for gas and border crossings. I drove past some of the grandest sights and most beautiful cities in the world, and never once thought of stopping to look. I drove the vehicle, but I was the one being driven. These were some of the strangest, most tormented hours of my life; and I still can't fully explain the swirling flood of emotion that seemed to be tearing me apart.

I found myself becoming deeply angry. I was mad at Dad, mad at God, mad at Ceausescu and every delusional Communist who dared think he had a clue about how to run a country; but I was ultimately mad at myself. I was in the pull of destiny and I knew it; but I seemed to think if I could put enough miles between me and those kids and that awful place, I could somehow get off the hook. So much happened on that long drive across the continent. God was working on my heart, preparing me for a journey that was to change everything about how I imagined my life and ministry would be.

Other things were happening, too. A "chance" meeting in a roadside restaurant put us in touch with some fellow ministers who would later play a huge role in events in Romania.

Then one very bad thing happened. Dad began to feel unwell, and shortly after we arrived back in his home in Peterhead, he suffered a heart attack. Dad was rushed to hospital and we spent some very anxious days praying he would pull through. The physical impact on his body was profound, and though he would soon return home, he was never quite as strong again after that.

When I left Romania, I was utterly determined never to go back, but by the time we made it across Europe, God had completely changed my heart. Just before Dad started to feel ill, I finally gave way to what I knew was a fresh calling from God on my life. Other than the fact that I wasn't going anywhere till I knew Dad was okay, if we'd had another truck loaded with supplies ready to go, I would have got in and driven straight back to that orphanage.

As it turned out, I did go back within just a few weeks, then again a few weeks after that, then several times a year for the next sixteen years. So far, I've been there over a hundred times. There are a million stories I'm not taking time to tell here, stories about precious little girls like Nicoletta who became in my heart like one of my own kids. One day, Nicoletta was misdiagnosed as mentally ill and sent to a far-off facility somewhere in rural Romania. She dropped into an abyss of bureaucratic lunacy, and I was never able to find her again. I hated Romania. I loved Romania.

There's another story that would take another entire book to tell properly. On my second visit, I found a little boy, three years old at the time. Andrew, as we would one day call him, lived in an upstairs room in the Timisoara orphanage. When I walked into the room on my second visit, all the other kids were screaming and trying to attract the attention of their new visitor, but Andrew just stood there quietly, looking as if in some way he understood that life was not supposed to be like this.

The instant I saw him, I knew he was to be part of our family. It took many months of prayer and we needed miracle after miracle to make it happen (including some help from those ministers we met on the road trip back from our first visit), but one day Andrew got on the plane back to America with my wife Chrissie and I. We adopted him and had the joy of watching him grow into an incredible young man. He is a dedicated Christian, determined to live his life for the glory of God; and he makes Chrissie and me proud every single day.

Of course, the events I'm describing here

in just a very few words took years to live out, one day at a time. Romania broke my heart and brought me indescribable joy all at the same time. We saw obstacle after obstacle, miracle after miracle. Our whole ministry, our family and everyone who is part of my life became irrevocably invested in this amazing, beautiful, horrific, infuriating place.

We went back year after year, bringing food, clothing, blankets, medicines, and other urgently needed supplies. We brought special gift packages for thousands of kids every Christmas. Andrew's orphanage was totally refurbished. We brought engineers from Scotland and installed a whole new sewer system. We replaced the metal, lead-painted cribs with new wooden ones. Finally, the awful stench of filth and death was dispelled and the orphanage became a clean, modern facility. The kids were warm, well-fed and hope became a part of their lives for the very first time. It got to the stage where I began to relax a little. Things were getting better. Maybe we could actually stop soon, safe in the knowledge that the kids were going to be okay. Then the phone rang again.

Dad was calling. By now, seven years had passed. Dad's health was a constant concern, but his interest and his desire to be involved in everything we did was not in any way diminished. "I'm going to fax you a newspaper article," he said.

The article was in the Daily Mail of London. The headline made my blood run cold. It read: "The Dying Rooms of Moldova!"

The reporter described how he went to Moldova as a sports reporter, assigned to cover a soccer match between Moldova and England in the World Cup group qualifying stages. Somehow, this reporter found himself away from the capital city where the match was being held. He was in a small village called Hincesti and, for whatever reason, he was taken to the local orphanage. He described conditions even worse than I'd seen on our first visits to Romania. Could anything be worse than that horror? Could anything be worse than the rank, filthy place in which those Romanian children once lived? I would not have thought so. But I was wrong.

Moldova was once part of Romania. In its complicated history, it became a republic of the U.S.S.R., one tiny corner of the once sprawling Soviet empire. After the breakup of the Soviet Union, many thought Moldova would re-integrate with Romania. They share a border, speak the same language and have centuries of historical connections. Instead, Moldovan politicians declared the tiny province to be an independent nation. They quickly became, by far, the poorest nation in all of Europe. Even today, while the capital city of Chisinau is showing signs of modernizing, taking a drive into the countryside is like stepping back in time. Many homes have no indoor plumbing, no electricity, no sign anywhere that the twenty-first century has arrived. Most of Moldova's population live in abject poverty, scraping a desperate living in what is, by any measure, a Third World nation in the heart of modern Europe.

And so there was Dad calling me once again. It was getting close to Christmas and I was due to leave within a few days to bring our annual delivery of thousands of Christmas packages for Romania's orphanages. "Don't stay with the trucks!" he urged. "The others can take care of those. Go up to Moldova and see what's really going on with the kids there."

This time I didn't even try to fight. But what Dad didn't tell me was that while Moldova was only one country further east, I had to drive hundreds of miles on tiny roads banked by shoulder-high snow. Nor did he tell me that my journey would take me across the Carpathian mountains on the worst, narrowest, windiest, most dangerous roads I've ever seen. Nowadays, they have metal barriers around the worst of the hairpin bends, but there was no such protection back then. I had rented a little Mitsubishi Galant at the Budapest airport, and though we drove on that mountain road for many nerve-wracking hours, we did not see one other vehicle the whole way across the Carpathians. I think I'm a pretty good driver and I've driven on frozen roads before, but these mountains had me terrified. I literally prayed my way around the sharp bends, stealing glances out my side window (when I dared), down on to a sheer drop with absolutely nothing between me and certain death if I couldn't keep that little car from slipping off the edge. The crunch of frozen, rutted ice and snow beneath the tires is a sound I don't think I'll ever forget.

Eventually, we made it over the mountains and through the border checkpoint into Moldova. About an hour from the border, we found the village of Hincesti. That was when I realized I was looking at something I didn't think was possible — a country that was in even worse shape than Romania.

I stood in the doorway of the very same orphanage the reporter had written about. The courtyard, the doorway, the merciless, bone-chilling wind blasting in my face... every detail of the moment is forever burned into my memory.

I scanned the buildings. It would be ridiculously kind to call the place a shambles. The windows were cracked, broken, or, in many cases, without any glass at all. The woodwork was visibly rotting; garbage piles dotted the courtyard. I've never seen such a grim, forbidding place in my life; and this was where they sent their children. Just a typical scenario if you happened to be a child living in an orphanage in this insane part of the world.

"Philip, it's cold," someone said. "Go inside!" I didn't want to. I knew we were about to start on the next chapter of this heartbreaking story and I didn't know if I could take it. The bitter wind stung my face once again. I grasped the door handle and turned it. Freezing cold as I was, my palms were sweating. I opened the door and walked into... Hell!

"My Name is Stella!"

The stench was sickeningly familiar. First impressions in that dank little foyer were appalling enough, but I knew worse was to come. An old man appeared. We shook hands and he told us his name was Mr. Ciubotari, the orphanage director. After a few minutes, he began leading us from room to dismal room. Though it was the middle of the day, every room was dark. Blankets were hung in front of the useless windows in a vain attempt to keep out the cold.

The children huddled together in one corner of whatever room they were in. It looked as if they were wearing every article of clothing they could find. They just sat there in those dark, dingy rooms, shivering, rocking themselves, staring into space, the living epitome of hopelessness.

The old man showed me the boiler room, and one more reason why the place was so cold was immediately obvious. There were three boilers, but only one was still working. These were supposed to be coal-fired boilers, but in the one that was still working, there was only a small, impotent looking flame coming from nothing more than a few twigs and some scrap wood. The director showed me the coal bunker... empty!

Then came mealtime. They ate what I can only call slop mixed with a few grains of rice. A grain or two of rice fell from a bowl, and I watched a young girl desperately lick those scraps straight off the table.

I thought it was as bad as it could get, but not yet. We went to Director Ciubotari's office. He asked me a question. "Have you ever watched a child freeze to death?"

I managed to stutter and stammer a reply. "No. No, I haven't."

What he said next still makes me weep. "Thirty children died here last year. So far this year, sixteen have died. They froze to death in their beds!"

I struggled to grasp the horror this old man was conveying with his matter-of-fact descriptions of tragedies that, to him, were just everyday life. I don't mean that he didn't care or didn't want it to be different; he just didn't have the means to do anything to change things.

Someone poked their head around the office door and a short conversation in Moldovan took place. What I heard him say next was, I think, the most surreal sentence I've ever heard. "Some of the children want to sing for you," he said.

I followed the director out of his office in a daze. This just couldn't be happening. It was almost the twenty-first century and we were in the heart of Europe. These kids were starving and freezing to death less than a day's drive from some of the most powerful economies in the world.

The director led me to a room that looked a bit like a classroom, where about twenty of the children had gathered. The children were again wrapped up in their coats and hats and scarves, still shivering, still freezing cold, but there was a difference here. They almost looked joyful, and a few were smiling as they began their impromptu concert. One of the orphanage workers was playing a battered old accordion, wheezing out some traditional Moldovan tunes. The pleasure the children derived from singing these simple songs was incredible to see. It occurred to me that back home, when our kids gather to sing or perform, we're always there, encouraging them, praising their efforts, telling them how great they did. Here, they had no one but themselves to sing to, except that today, a few strangers were visiting, and they were ecstatic at the opportunity of performing for a real audience.

I smiled politely through the unfamiliar music. To be honest, I was hoping that it would be over quickly. We had things to do. I was touched by their desperate circumstances and I knew that we would help all we could, but, apparently, I still wasn't sufficiently "on the hook" as far as God was concerned. In my spirit, I felt Him speak to me: "If you won't touch them, I'll make them touch you!"

Just then, I heard a song so familiar that anyone who has ever been in church would recognize it within four notes. In the midst of this hell-hole, I heard those cold, starving, tortured children begin singing praises to God! They were singing, "This is the day! This is the day that the Lord has made!" Then came a line that instantly brought tears to my eyes. "We will rejoice! We will rejoice and be glad in it…"

They were in a black hole of poverty and hopelessness, yet still they could sing, still they could find enough spirit within themselves to "be glad and rejoice" in the day that the Lord had made. I looked at their faces, and suddenly they weren't just poor kids in awful circumstances. I'd been telling myself, "Treat it like it's a video, like you're just watching something on TV." But I wasn't going to get away with being a spectator any longer. I was right there, I was in the middle of their suffering, and if their pain continued, I was no longer innocent. I couldn't blame the communists, or the bureaucracy, or the director or the staff. If their pain continued, it would be my fault.

I dried my eyes as best I could and began

to join with them in their concert. I was only thirteen-years old when I started traveling with Dad on his ministry trips. He would preach while I sang and played the accordion. At least the right instrument was available, so I borrowed the old accordion and began to sing and play with the children. Somewhere over the course of those few songs we sang together, I stopped noticing my heart knitting to theirs. I stopped caring that the more I got to know them, the more they were going to become my responsibility. If they could live the desperate lives they were living and still sing and praise God, what right did I have to complain about having to do a bit more work than I'd planned?

After we finished singing, I began talking to the kids with the help of my Romanian friend and colleague, Viorel Soter. We call him Vio for short, and he is my guide, interpreter, troubleshooter — you name it, Vio takes cares of it. We met Vio when I was in the process of adopting Andrew. Andrew's biological father had disappeared from the scene and his birth-mother, Dana, had begun to date Vio. God was surely guiding our steps, but I had no way of knowing back then that this young couple would one day become fast friends and join me in our ministry to these children. Vio has lived a hard life, struggling through the worst of the poverty and hardship that communism and dictatorship inflicted on the people of Romania. Vio is a genuinely good man, but he has seen enough corruption and brutality in his life to have developed a strong sense of skepticism and he is not an emotional person at all. But even Vio's tough exterior could not mask his feelings as he relayed the stories of the lives these children were forced to live. Vio's tears flowed along with mine, and we all knew we were going to be in this for the long haul. We weren't going anywhere till these kids were safe and properly cared for.

As we sang together, I had noticed one of

the girls on the front row. Her right forearm was badly deformed and curled outward from her body, stiff and almost useless. She seemed to be the oldest of the kids, and the other kids clearly thought of her as their leader. We began to talk and I knew right away that we were going to be friends.

"My name is Stella," she told me.

Stella and I spent a long, wonderful time just chatting and getting to know more about each other. Her full name was Stella Bivol, and she had been living at the Hincesti orphanage for two years. She told me that her father left home in 1992, and her mother was left with no choice but to put Stella, her two sisters and her three brothers in the care of the orphanage system.

Stella asked me about my family, so I told her about Chrissie, who wasn't with us on that trip, and about our four children. She asked about our home, the town we lived in, how long it took to travel to Moldova and what seemed like a million other questions. It was as though she had been saving up questions that she would ask someone from the outside if she ever got the chance. Her chance had finally come, and she wasn't going to miss a moment. She was dealing with some major disabilities, including epilepsy and malformations of her arm and leg. There was nothing wrong with her mind, however, and she soaked in every detail of our conversation.

After a while she asked, "Would you come with me, please?"

We followed Stella to what the children call the salon, that is, the dormitory where they slept and kept whatever personal belongings they had. Stella pulled out a little bag and emptied it out on her bed. She had two small embroidered tapestries, and a meager little sewing kit.

"She made these herself," said one of the orphanage workers.

Stella proudly showed me the two little tapestries she had created, each one about two feet square.

"They are beautiful," I told her.

She beamed as I used the little bit of Moldovan I could speak to tell her what an awesome job she had done. Considering she only had one good hand, it really was an incredible achievement.

Then that young girl did something that literally took my breath away. In all my life, I've rarely witnessed such an act of spontaneous, unselfish generosity.

"You take this one!" she said. "I want to give it to you!"

Then Stella handed me one of her two tapestries. In a world where teens have their own cell phones and iPods and PlayStations, her gift might not seem like much to some people, but out of a life of utter poverty, Stella had just given me half of all she possessed. All she had that was purely her own were those two tapestries, and she had just given away half of what she loved most.

Stella didn't know it, but she had just ensured and confirmed that she had become "mine," my responsibility, my job to take care of. I looked at her little bit of thread and her two or three well-used sewing needles. Next time I came back — and by now there was no doubt there would be a next time — I promised myself that Stella would find herself with more thread and material and sewing accessories than she would know what to do with.

I hugged Stella and carefully folded her gift over my arm, where it stayed all day. I still have it, and it remains one of my most precious possessions.

Officially, the orphanage at Hincesti was designed to house children with disabilities. Some of the kids were wheelchair-bound, one little girl was totally blind and many of the kids had severe developmental issues. All I knew is that within the first few hours after I met them,

God had knitted my heart to theirs, and I knew that neither their lives nor mine would ever be the same.

The first problem we needed to solve was the danger from the freezing cold temperatures. It was daylight now and there wasn't a warm corner in the entire place. That night, I knew the temperature would plummet well below zero. I couldn't get the old man's words out of my head. "Thirty children died here last year. So far this year, sixteen have died..."

As I have now discovered many times, the combination of poorly functioning heating systems and broken bedroom windows will kill children. Either problem is a major one, but when both are in place at the same time, kids are going to die. The director told me that one night, it was so cold that he crammed all the children into one salon for the night. By morning, seven of the children were dead. Kids like my new friend, Stella, might not make it through the freezing nights ahead! I asked Vio how much cash it would take to get us to Hungary (where I could use my credit cards again), and we left all the money we could spare.

We had a major job to do, but I was out of time and out of funds. We had just spent a small fortune getting Christmas gifts to thousands of children in Romania and we just hadn't budgeted for taking on the care of two hundred more children plus the repair and upkeep of a whole orphanage. I left the children at Hincesti knowing I was about to make my fastest ever round-trip home to America and back again to Moldova. I flew home, took care of the commitments I had there, told as many people as I could and gathered as much funds and supplies as I knew how to in just a couple of weeks. Every day away was spent praying that the weather would not be too bad, that those children would survive through the brutally cold Moldovan nights.

I got my Dad to get together a truckload of supplies, but all our drivers were tied up. At such short notice, all we could do was find someone who was at least able to get the truck the first twelve hours or so to London. I then had to fly in, meet the truck in London and drive the rest of the three-day journey to Moldova myself. It was our only option, so that's what we did.

We finally found a coal supplier. That day was a public holiday, so I literally had to get the owner to leave his home and open up the depot. Eventually, we were able to get a load of coal delivered. The one working boiler was filled with coal and the insipid flame from the twigs was replaced by a glowing, roaring fire. For the first time since I arrived in Moldova, I felt actual heat. I stood by the boiler and almost wept for joy. It took a while, but the system gradually began to get enough heat through the ancient metal radiators to take a little of the chill out of the air. I later learned that on its best day, the boiler only worked at 65% capacity, but that was enough for now.

It was a simple enough thing to do, costing around eighteen hundred dollars for a month's worth of coal, but that one act alone broke the cycle of death in that orphanage. They had innumerable problems, and we would need to make many more frantic interventions over time, but by simply making sure they never ran out of coal, we took the horrible prospect of freezing to death out of the equation. Not one single child has frozen to death in the Hincesti orphanage since we sent in that first load of coal.

"Can We Call You Daddy?"

Stella became my best friend. I know that sounds odd, but she quickly became as much a friend to me as anyone ever has. Every time I went back to the Hincesti orphanage, she was the first one I looked for. She became my "guide," telling me all about what was happening in the other kids' lives, explaining everything that had happened since my last visit, and pointing me to any of the kids who happened to need just a little extra attention. Just a young girl with a million reasons to give in to hopelessness, Stella stayed strong, optimistic and ever supportive of the other children in the orphanage.

We sent truckloads of supplies, made sure the orphanage never ran out of coal until a new oil-fired system was installed, and then we made sure they never ran out of oil. I went there several times a year, and visiting with Stella and the other kids became as important to me as anything in my life. I especially loved Christmas time. My dad made sure that the volunteers in Scotland prepared a truck for Moldova, in addition to the trucks that were already being sent to Romania. At Christmas time, I let the team from Scotland handle Romania, and I always took the truck for Moldova myself. Loaded with thousands of Christmas gifts, for kids in orphanages all over Moldova, I made my way across those same Carpathian mountains. By the time we reached Moldova, I was always bursting with anticipation to see the excitement on the faces of the kids when we brought them their gifts.

I think (actually, I know), I got a bigger kick out of giving out those gifts than the kids got receiving them. I would sit on the floor for hours as child after child brought me their package and showed me what they had received. I'd play with them, laugh with them, and marvel that a few toys put inside a shoe box and wrapped in Christmas paper could make a child forget he was an orphan and feel like a normal kid, at least for one day a year.

As always, when we got to Hincesti, Stella

helped "supervise" the distribution of the gifts, taking me by the hand and leading me from salon to salon where the kids were waiting for their gifts. It was quite simply the best day of their year. As elated as the children were, I don't have words to describe the sheer joy I felt in my own heart, that I was able to play a part in making those incredible days possible.

Over the years, as we kept up our regular visits to Hincesti, I noticed that other organizations were helping there as well. The facility was gradually being rebuilt and modernized. It was a far different place than we first found, and it seemed certain that the kids would never again be in the peril they faced when I first found them. I began to relax. I planned to keep going back, especially at Christmas time, but I began to feel that perhaps I was free to move on to other things. In my mind, I was already planning for the changes we would make back in our ministry in America, now that we could focus less on overseas work. At our headquarters near Montgomery, Alabama, we had opened Brigadoon, a Christian camp and conference center that was providing life-changing ministry to children, youth and families, and I was keen to expand that effort as much as possible.

That's about what I was thinking as I drove our vehicle to an orphanage in the town of Leova. We'd been to Hincesti and I'd had a wonderful Christmas with Stella and the kids there. We'd delivered gifts to some other orphanages, and now I was about to make our last stop for that year. I'd never been to the Leova orphanage, but I knew they had about four hundred children there who would be glad to receive their Christmas presents.

On our way down the main road from Hincesti to Leova, we passed a little blue sign pointing down a dirt track off to the right side of the road. One of the team that was with us that year was Tom Valley, a doctor from Columbus,

Ohio. He spotted the sign and read the Moldovan words, "Casa de Copii Orfani." Literally, it translates as "House for Orphan Children."

I knew what Tom was going to say next. "There's an orphanage down there. Let's go visit the kids."

"We can't, Tom," I answered. "I've already promised gifts to the kids in Leova and they're waiting for us. I don't know if I have enough gift packages as it is. Anyway, we don't have a lot of time. We need to get finished and get started back if we're going to make our flight home."

Actually, I said a lot more, and as Tom kept trying to persuade me, I got a little upset with him. We kept going and got to the orphanage in Leova. I enjoyed being with the kids, and I was glad to see that their facility, while far from luxurious, was sound enough to provide good shelter. The children looked well cared for, and it seemed like they were getting enough food. This particular orphanage was being sponsored by Moldova's Prime Minister, so apparently, that attention was enough to ensure that the director was at least given enough resources for food and building repairs.

Tired and happy to be done for that trip, we started back towards Hincesti and the road out of Moldova. Soon we were approaching that blue sign again. Tom started pleading all over again. "Please, let's go see what's down there."

It's alright for you, I thought to myself. You'll get back on the plane to America and I'll probably never see you again. If I go down there, I could be on the hook all over again. I felt myself already losing the familiar battle.

Nevertheless, I turned the van I was driving onto the gravel road, and we stopped and got out of the vehicles. On this trip, the truck from Scotland was driven by Willie Moffatt, a gruff, no-nonsense Scotsman. On this rare occasion, Willie had driven the truck all the way from Scotland, relieving me of the need to drive it myself this trip. "Willie," I pleaded, "you see the state of that road. It's a mud pile — there's no way we can get the truck down there, is there?"

Willie totally missed my cue. "Oh, I think we'll be alright," he said. "You go in front with the van and if I see you in trouble I can stay back and tow you out."

I like Willie, but right then I could have hit him with a two-by-four. But Willie is a tough ex-soldier, and, as I've joked since, taking him on while he could see me coming definitely wasn't an option. I was getting no help from the rest of the team either, who all seemed inexplicably ready to go exploring the remotest possible reaches of the Moldovan countryside. With that, we continued down the little mud track and, as remote as we already were, plunged into the middle of nowhere.

We continued down the mud track, slithering in and out of deep ruts and, for all of

Willie's initial confidence, I later learned even he thought we might be in trouble. We reached a fork in the road. There were no other signs, either to the orphanage, or to whatever town or village in which it was supposed to be. I pretty much mentally flipped a coin and took the fork to the right. The road got even worse and Tom looked more sheepish by the minute.

If I could have found a spot wide enough to turn around I would have done it and got out of there. We slid and slithered on for miles and I was getting genuinely fearful that we might get completely stuck. We hadn't seen a soul since we turned off the main road and there was no telling how long it would be before someone found us, nor how friendly they would be when they got there.

It was starting to get dark when I finally saw a building up ahead. It was a large building, and just past it we could see a few houses. This, we would discover, was the village of Cupcui, and that large building was the orphanage we'd been looking for.

I know I've described this feeling before, but as I approached the rickety old door leading into the orphanage, I already knew once again that my world was about to change. First the orphanage in Timisoara, then the orphanage in Hincesti, and now here in this tiny corner of oblivion, all were doors through which once entered, there was no going back.

Every word I've said about Timisoara and Hincesti could be applied to Cupcui, but even those tragic places didn't match up to this. Yes, there was the same stench of filth and death and despair, the same lonely, fearful little faces, and the same constant struggle just to survive another day. But I literally don't have the words to describe how desperately awful this place was. I look at pictures today and I still weep. People are kinder to their animals than these kids were being treated.

I walked into bedrooms where the walls were covered — literally covered — with a vile looking black mold. Kids slept inches from this disease-ridden fungus. The roof was failing hopelessly. "When it rains outside for a day, it rains inside for a week!" they told me.

There were no toilets in the building, nowhere to bathe. To relieve themselves, the children had to trek to a distant outhouse. There was no toilet or toilet paper in there, just a hole in the ground. We learned later that the buildup of untreated waste had tainted the well supplying water to the orphanage. They were drinking poison. Another outhouse provided the only place to bathe in the whole facility — a single, disgusting looking shower stall, with holes in the walls open to the outside. Children were given one five-minute shower once a week in freezing cold water. And, once again, a failing heating system and cracked, broken windows put kids' lives at risk every single night.

As Christians, we're supposed to forgive people. We're supposed to love our neighbor. We're even supposed to love our enemy. But each time I am greeted by such despicable neglect, such sickening filth, such despair and hopelessness in the faces of tiny, defenseless children, all I can feel is rage. I've looked into the faces of certain officials, stunned by their apathy, sickened by their greed as they've tried to squeeze a bribe from me, just to let me go help the kids they're supposed to be responsible for; and it has taken every shred of self-control I possess not to rip their throats out. I'm sorry if that doesn't sound very Christian, yet I cannot imagine God feeling anything less than profound anger when He sees the cruelty inflicted upon these children.

There were eighty children in the Cupcui orphanage, from age four to age sixteen. No one in the world, it seemed, even knew they existed. If they knew, they certainly didn't care. I walked in to a room and some kids were having a Christmas concert – for other kids. No one was there to watch them perform, so they watched each other. I remembered the kids singing to me on that first day in Hincesti, and here I was again with kids that had not a single soul who wanted to come and hear their songs, applaud their efforts, and tell them how well they had done. They had just finished, so I asked them to start over. Our team sat down and the kids beamed with excitement as they went through their program all over again, but this time with an actual audience.

As I sat there listening to them, I tried to figure out where to start. We'd have to fix the roof, install toilets and showers and get a new heating system. I soon realized that to do everything needed, we'd basically have to rebuild the whole place from the ground up.

"This is huge," I prayed. "We're not big enough to take this on. We can't do it!"

I don't know how you feel about people who tell you God talks to them. God has many ways of communicating to us, of course. As we read the Bible, as we view the wonders of creation, as we listen to someone preach, in fact in any of the normal things we do every day, we can sense the direction and leading of God for our lives. But, sometimes, I believe He can also interrupt our thoughts, invade our circumstances, and place His direct instructions into our spirit.

"We can't do it!" I told Him.

"But I can!" He replied.

More clearly and precisely than if someone had stood six inches from my ear and said the words out loud, I heard His voice in my spirit that day. He said something else as well. He didn't just want me to help them, feed them, and make sure they had a decent place to live. He wanted me much more involved than that…

"I want you to make them like your own

children. I want you to be a father to them!"

And so began our great adventure in Cupcui. Over the next few months, we saw incredible miracles as God was true to His word and provided the means to rebuild that orphanage. It took hundreds of thousands of dollars and more faith and more prayer than I ever thought I had in me, but in less than a year, that ghastly, awful place was transformed into a modern, warm, comfortable, safe home for "my kids."

We built a new roof over the old flat roof and not only stopped the incessant leaking, but created a whole new floor that we turned into recreation rooms for each of the different age groups. We got rid of the mold-covered walls. We put beautiful, modern showers and toilets on each floor — no more outhouses. We replaced the ancient heating system with a modern system capable of heating the whole orphanage from top to bottom. We installed a water purification system so the water supply would no longer make the kids sick. New carpets, new beds, new paint... new everything!

But rebuilding the orphanage was only the start. Those kids really did become mine. I got to know them more closely than any of the kids we'd ever been involved with. Liuda, Marina, Dorin, Rodica, Irina and scores more, all became fixed in my heart. God really was making me a father to them. And when they met my wife Chrissie, it was literally love at first sight. We were there every few weeks, and as much as I missed home, I missed Cupcui just as much when we weren't there.

One day, Chrissie and I were chatting to some kids when Marina, one of the older girls, motioned to me to come over. I went to her and she said that a group of the children wanted me to come upstairs so they could ask me a question. I followed Marina upstairs and wondered what they could possibly want. They were all waiting in a huddle and they pointed to the chair in the middle of the room. I sat, mystified, nervous.

"What do your children call you?" one of them asked.

"They call me Dad," I told them.

And Chrissie, what do they call her?"

"They call her Mom."

They started whispering to each other, then Marina said, "Can we do the same? Can we call Chrissie Mom? Can we call you Dad?"

It doesn't happen often, but I was speechless. I was told to be a father to them, and now they were asking me themselves if I would be exactly that. Choking back tears, I assured them that I would be thrilled to have them think of Chrissie and me as their mom and dad. It sure made for a big family, but somehow, we never ran out of room in our hearts for these precious, beautiful children.

Stella was one of the first orphans Philip Cameron met in Moldova. She suffered from epilepsy and had a deformity in her left arm and hand. Despite the obstacles she faced, she was a natural leader who selflessly looked out for the well-being of the other children. Her tragic death from AIDS after being forced into prostitution upon leaving the orphanage, showed Philip the urgent need for a place like Stella's House.

Below: Stella's House No.1. Located in Moldova's capital city, Chisinau, this home and other Stella's Houses provide safety and care for girls who must leave the orphanages at age sixteen.

Above: As the serving United States Ambassador to Moldova at the time, Michael D. Kirby (center) joined Philip and others to officially open Stella's House No. 1.

Below: Philip and Chrissie Cameron with some of the girls from Stella's House.

Above: The girls talk with Philip and share their stories during a recent visit to a church in the United States.

Below: Constantia returns to the orphanage to share hope and help just as others once shared it with her. Constantia and Galina have made regular visits back to the Cupcui orphanage to hold Bible studies and provide other encouragement and help to the children.

Above: April 2009 — United States Ambassador to Moldova, Asif J. Chaudhry, cuts the ribbon to open Stella's House No.2.

Below: Stella's House No. 2 is seen on the right, along with the almost-complete Stella's 3 in the foreground (ready for use as of early 2010). On the far side of this picture, land and a home shell have already been acquired to begin work on Stella's House No. 4.

"Where is Stella?"

Things in Cupcui were coming along well. The buildings had been transformed and I knew that whatever happened now, we would make sure the children would be okay. We still helped the other orphanages, but most of our time was now being spent in Cupcui. Though I no longer had my dad pushing me on — he went home to the Savior he loved so much in September of 2002 — I knew that what had been accomplished in Cupcui would have brought him immense joy.

We had to drive by the Hincesti orphanage on our way to Cupcui, so I often had the chance to drop by and see Stella and the other kids there. The facility at Hincesti was unrecognizable as the place we first found. This was no longer home to "The Dying Rooms of Moldova!" Those early newspaper stories had done the trick and some large European organizations had gotten involved. Between what we did initially and what these folks were now doing, the children in Hincesti had been rescued from certain disaster.

Every Christmas, we still went to orphanages all over the country with thousands of Christmas packages. That time had come again, and I was looking forward to seeing all the kids and enjoying my favorite time of year with them once again.

We pulled up with our truck into the courtyard at Hincesti and the children recognized us immediately. They knew what was coming and they were ready for Christmas.

"Pheelip, Pheelip," they screamed.

Other than a few new arrivals, I knew every one of those kids by name. One thing they could certainly do was put on a welcome, and it was a long time before I got through greeting all the children. Finally, I went inside and looked for the Director. Soon we got organized and we began getting the truck unloaded with all the gift packages for the children. After that I got ready to make the rounds of all the rooms as the children opened their gifts. But something was seriously wrong. By now, Stella would have usually firmly attached herself to me, and would be guiding me from room to room as she always did. At first I thought she might have been busy somewhere inside and she simply hadn't noticed that we'd arrived. But it was Christmas, and normally every kid in the place knew within seconds that we were there with their gifts.

The orphanage had its own in-house doctor, and I spotted her as I went down the hall. "Dr. Liudmila... Unde Stella? (Where is Stella?)"

Looking more than a little uncomfortable, she turned to Vio and told him a very long story in Moldovan. I watched his face turn whiter with every word. I know enough of the language that normally, I can pick up most of what is said, but on this occasion, I was totally lost; but I knew enough to know that I was about to get some bad news.

"Stella is gone," Vio told me. "She is too old to stay here, and they moved her to another place. They were bad to her, and she ran away. Now no one knows where she is."

I don't often get angry with the people who work in the orphanages. I know they do hard, sometimes impossible work, but I began asking Dr. Liudmila some very pointed questions.

"Why did no one tell me she was being moved?" You know I would have made sure she was okay. When did this happen? Where did they send her? What did they do that made her run away?"

On and on I went. I pressed the director for answers as well. I was not happy that they hadn't tried to let me know in advance and, for the first time since I went to Hincesti, they weren't too happy to have to talk to me. We gave the children their gifts, but I was still boiling with rage. I always loved Christmas, but I could find no joy this time.

When we left I spoke to Vio about the situation. "I will try to find her. When we are finished with the Christmas presents, I will search for her," he said.

Vio was true to his word. He ended up in Transnistria, a breakaway region of Moldova with loyalties to Russia. It's a dangerous, lawless part of the world and a haven for organized crime. Vio heard rumors, and people claimed to have seen her, but he was never able to find Stella. The rumor that disturbed me most was that Stella had been seen working as a prostitute. They told Vio that Stella worked the streets of Tiraspol in Transnistria, and was used by filthy men in ways I cannot put on paper.

Vio continued his search, but to no avail.

Months went by without any news, and my heart continued to break for my friend Stella. I went back and forth to Moldova every few weeks, each time hoping to hear something, hoping for some miracle to help me find Stella.

Then, finally, the awful words were spoken. I went back again to Hincesti, and asked if they had any news. In that cold, matter-of-fact way that the workers in the orphanage have developed, Dr. Liudmila announced, "Stella mourit! (Stella is dead!)"

Then, Dr. Liudmila pronounced three letters, but phonetically, as a single word: "HIV." Stella had contracted AIDS and died. Vile men used that precious little girl until they killed her.

I could tell you how stunned I was, how stricken with grief I was over the fate of my beautiful friend, and that would all be true. I could try to describe the palpable despair and sorrow that engulfed my soul at that moment, and I'm sure you would share in that sorrow. But as real and valid as all that is, the real tragedy is in the needlessness of it all. I just can't come to terms with the callousness and systemic wickedness that permitted such an awful thing to happen to anyone, let alone someone as vulnerable, yet decent, generous and kind as Stella. In my nightmares, I still see her last hours of life, wracked with pain, stricken with terror and, worst of all, totally alone.

Stella's death still tears at my heart. I know that in our visits to Hincesti, Stella heard the gospel message many times. I am certain she understood the love that Jesus had for her that drove Him to the cross for her. I truly believe she knew Jesus as her Savior and Lord and I pray His presence brought her comfort in her final days. But no one should have to endure a fate like that. Stella's death was utterly preventable, and that is a thought that haunts me every day of my life.

In the months that followed Stella's

disappearance, I came to grasp two horrific truths. One was that every year, when kids reach the age of sixteen, they are removed from the orphanages. The Government is supposed to make provision for them, but when kids don't show up where they are supposed to after leaving the orphanages, the Government does not have the resources — or the will — to go find them. Instead, what usually happens is that the child leaves the orphanage after their sixteenth birthday and, as far as officialdom is concerned, just disappears. They leave the orphanage with a few dollars and a bus ticket to whatever town appears on their papers, and with that, at sixteen years of age, they are on their own.

With few options, the young girls are especially prone to suffering Stella's fate. They end up selling themselves on the streets just to survive. Then there are the traffickers. Moldova has been called the engine of the sex industry. Every year, when the orphanages send out the young girls after they become sixteen, the traffickers lie in wait. Most of the bus services from outlying areas use the capital city of Chisinau as a hub. No matter where a young girl's ultimate destination is, she will probably need to change buses in Chisinau. The traffickers know this, and you can often see their fancy cars lining up when the buses come in. Some corrupt orphanage workers will even alert the criminals when a "suitable" young girl is on her way.

The traffickers know exactly who to look for, and they soon begin to spin stories of good jobs in exotic locations. They talk of earning hundreds of dollars a week while working as a nanny or in classy restaurants. They weave their lies together so convincingly that these naïve young orphans soon willingly turn themselves over to the traffickers. They climb into those fancy cars, and are never seen again.

Michael D. Kirby, while serving as the United States Ambassador to Moldova, told me this: "Within twenty-four hours of getting into a car, they are in places like Turkey or Saudi Arabia or Italy." They are beaten, raped and brutalized until they comply with the wishes of their new masters. They are slaves in every sense of the word, sold on to other buyers for two or three thousand dollars. They will perform sexual services for eager customers as much as thirty times a day — or suffer the consequences. Ultimately, through mistreatment, disease and neglect, many will die just as Stella did.

The second horror that gripped me was the realization that we had just invested years of our lives and an enormous amount of money making Cupcui a safe place for young girls who now called Chrissie and me Mom and Dad. And there were other young girls in orphanages all over Moldova in places like Leova and Straseni and Hincesti, filled with hundreds of girls that we knew and cared for. But all of them would only be safe until they were sixteen. Then what?

How could we allow the same thing to happen to them as happened to Stella? How could we allow these beautiful young ladies to fall into the hands of evil men who would sell them into sexual slavery? If the phrase, "Over my dead body!" comes to mind, you know my response to those questions.

I spent a lot of time talking to officials. I mean hours, days and weeks of my life were spent smiling, pleading, coaxing and cajoling people whose job it was supposed to be to take care of these kids in the first place. I don't want to name names, but while many were typically apathetic, others were genuinely helpful.

As the discussions unfolded, it soon became clear that we needed to get a "refuge house" where the kids could go when they were finished at the orphanage. We bought a small cottage near the Cupcui orphanage, and at first this seemed like a potential solution. We were allowed to take the kids from the orphanage there to visit, and we'd rotate through about ten different kids every day that we were there. It certainly helped cement our relationship with the children, and we were able to give them a taste of what life was like outside an orphanage. It was and remains a great place to bring the kids.

These days, this is our "mission house" where teams of volunteer helpers can live while they help us in Moldova. But this still wasn't solving the problem of what happened after the children reached sixteen years of age. While our little house in the village had room for a dozen kids, we ran straight into a bureaucratic brick wall.

The same people who never had a thing to say when young girls simply disappeared at the hands of traffickers, suddenly found lots of ways to be involved when we offered to provide those girls with round-the-clock care in a safe, secure home.

We couldn't do it, they told us. How did

they know we wouldn't take the kids overseas and sell their body parts to hospitals in the west? How did they know we weren't secret sex-traffickers ourselves? We eventually had to deal with officials at the local, regional and national levels, each meeting seemingly more outrageous and insane than the last.

But every now and then, a little glimmer of common sense and compassion broke through the red tape. Finally, a word of wisdom straight from Heaven broke the deadlock. It was a simple thing, something we had intended to implement from the start, but only God knew when to bring it forth.

"Of course," I told the assembled officials, "we want to make sure the cycle of poverty is broken, so that these girls never have to resort to selling themselves on the streets. We want them to learn job skills. We would teach them English (a marketable skill in itself). Some of these kids are incredibly smart and they need to go on to University. It's vital that they complete their education."

I had just said the word that provided these officials with a basis for approving our plans — education! After many more hours of discussion, they hammered out the rules by which girls who left the orphanage would be able to stay in our house. They could only stay there if we took complete legal responsibility for them. We had to have someone certified by the Moldovan government as the primary director of the house. (That condition could have killed the whole arrangement, but we'd already invited the Deputy Director of the Cupcui orphanage to be on our staff.) And, finally, we had to make sure the girls stayed in school or in vocational training. As long as they were in school or in training, they could stay at our house.

There was just one problem. The only house we had was near the orphanage. The schools and training courses the girls needed to attend were all in the capital city of Chisinau, a ninety minute drive away. There was only one thing to do — we would have to buy a house in Chisinau!

Our small non-profit organization doesn't exactly have much of a reserve. When we get enough money to fix an orphanage or buy new beds for kids or whatever it is that's needed, we spend that money. I travel and preach and tell people what we are doing in Moldova. People hear about it and help, and that's pretty much where our funding has come from. There have been times when I didn't see how we could possibly do all that we had before us to do, but I give God all the glory for miracle after miracle that has made the impossible come to pass before our eyes. And when I tell you that coming up with hundreds of thousands of dollars to buy a house in Moldova was going to take a miracle, believe me, I am using the word in its most literal sense.

The way builders work in Moldova is that they will construct a shell—just walls and a roof. You can see those unfinished homes all over Moldova. People then buy that shell and either hire a builder to do the rest of the construction or do the work themselves. I spoke to the builder who had done the rebuilding work for us at the Cupcui orphanage, and he directed me to several properties he knew of in Chisinau. It had to be big enough that it could be set up to house about twenty girls plus staff. It also had to be easy to secure. We looked at several houses, then we turned down one of the muddiest streets in the entire city of Chisinau. Sometimes you just know that God has gone before you to prepare exactly what you need, and that's what I knew as soon as I saw the house on Str. Sperantei — or in English — the house on Hope Street!

The house was big enough, it was reasonably isolated from passing traffic, and it had a huge security wall around the property. It was absolutely tailor-made for our purposes.

Having found it, we needed to purchase it and then pay for the construction needed to make it ready to live in. It took many months and many miracles before we were done. People gave to buy the house, then others gave to do the construction work. We made a huge list of everything you need to live in a home—right down to the salt and pepper shakers. We put that list on a registry in several online stores and people all over America helped buy the furniture and the drapes and the bedding and knives and forks. Finally, we put all that aboard a forty-foot container and shipped it to Moldova. There were more than a few hiccups, delays and disappointments along the way, but finally the house was finished! I will never forget the day we brought those girls to their new home. I wept, they wept, we all rejoiced and thanked God for his faithfulness in providing this beautiful place of safety.

I looked around at the girls who were there. Liudmila (Liuda), Constantia, the two Marinas (one of whom was nicknamed Bobocelli), Felicia, Olga, Rodica and others. I'd known them now for three years and they were all truly precious to me. Now they were safe. Now we wouldn't watch them grow and care for them every day, only to lose them forever just because they turned sixteen. I had lost Stella, but I would lose no more of them.

As we prayed and dedicated that house, Stella filled all our thoughts. It was her life and her death that had brought us to this place. This house was built so that these precious young orphan girls need never suffer the way Stella suffered. There was never any doubt what we would call it. This was Stella's House!

Philip Cameron
As told to Brian Paterson
Philip Cameron Ministries

AFTERWORD

As of 2010, Philip Cameron Ministries has purchased and built more Stella's Houses, so that he is now working on a fourth safe house for the orphan girls in Moldova. The first orphans he saved like Natalie, Galina, Constantia, Dasa and Irina, now help operate these houses, helping the new orphans who come to Stella's Houses feel welcome and safe. Holding Bible studies for the younger girls and helping them reach their education goals, the girls show the orphans that God loves them, and they are special.

In an amazing turn of events, the Moldovan Government has requested that Philip Cameron Ministries completely take over the running of the Cupcui facility starting in January, 2010, and operate it as a private orphanage. This brings a weighty responsibility as the government will no longer be providing any financial support to the orphanage, but this is also an incredible opportunity to care for the children in a nurturing Christian environment, impacting their lives in ways that simply were not possible until now.

You can help these children by contributing to Philip Cameron Ministries at the address below.

Philip Cameron Ministries
P.O. Box 241241
Montgomery, AL 36124
www.philip-cameron.org

ABOUT PHILIP CAMERON

Philip's introduction to ministry came at the early age of thirteen, traveling and singing with his father, Evangelist Simon Peter Cameron. In 1974, the two began Faith Acres Bible School in their home town of Peterhead, Scotland. This endeavor has developed into a multi-faceted ministry center now known as The New Hope Trust.

Philip has written four books on Household Salvation, and he is deeply passionate about helping Christians win their loved ones to Christ. Brigadoon, near Montgomery, Alabama, opened in 1996, and is home to a beautiful Campground and Family Ministry Center. Focused on reaching children and families, Brigadoon plays a vital role in the ministry's primary mission: ***Connecting Your Family to God... Connecting You to God's Family!***

Philip began helping Romania's orphans in 1990, then extended this work to neighboring Moldova. After the tragic death of a young orphan called Stella, Philip opened a refuge home called Stella's House in 2006. Like Stella, many young girls are forced out of Moldova's orphanages at age sixteen and become easy prey for Moldova's rampant sex-trafficking industry. Stella's Houses provide nurture, education, a safe living environment, and the opportunity to experience the love of Jesus in action on a daily basis.

Philip has been married to his hometown sweetheart, Chrissie, since 1976. Philip and Chrissie live in Montgomery, Alabama, where they have raised four children: Philip, Melody Joy, Andrew and Lauren Anne.

ABOUT BRIAN PATERSON

A 1978 graduate of the Bible College the Cameron family began in Peterhead, Scotland, Brian continued working with Philip Cameron and traveled the world as part of *The Camerons* singing group and ministry team. Today, Brian is a senior director of Philip Cameron Ministries. Brian is a gifted writer who has helped numerous well-known ministers create books based on their sermons and teaching series. Brian lives in Montgomery, Alabama with his wife, Yvonne, and their three children, Brian, Jr., James and Sarah.

ABOUT NANCY SILVERS

Nancy Silvers is the author of Script A Life personal history books. Having taught writing for over twenty years and being a published author herself, Nancy believes the most important stories to tell are our own. Mother of three sons and "Nana" to three precious grandchildren, Nancy understands the value of recording personal memories.

A portion of proceeds from each story she writes goes to Stella's House, a ministry close to her heart. Nancy lives in Ponte Vedra Beach, Florida.

Script A Life
35 Players Club Villas
Ponte Vedra Beach, Florida 32082
Scriptalife.com